Books by Enrique Hank Lopez

MY BROTHER LYNDON, *Sam Houston Johnson*
  *with Enrique Hank Lopez*
AFRO-SIX
LA BALSA, Vital Alsar,
  *as told to Enrique Hank Lopez*
HIGHEST HELL
SEVEN WIVES OF WESTLAKE
THE HARVARD MYSTIQUE

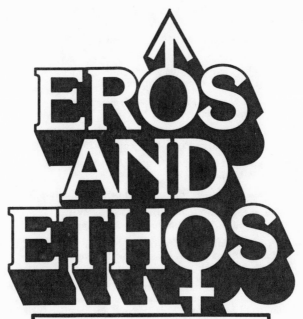

# EROS AND ETHOS

## A Comparative Study of Catholic, Jewish and Protestant Sex Behavior

Enrique Hank Lopez

PRENTICE-HALL, INC., Englewood Cliffs, N.J.

The author expresses appreciation for permission to reprint excerpts or quotations from the following works:

"On Knowing," by Jerome Bruner, 1962. Used by permission of Harvard University Press.

Quotation from "The View from the Back of the Shul," by Audrey Gellis. Used by permission of Audrey Gellis, copyright Audrey Gellis.

*Helping People: Karen Horney's Psychoanalytic Approach*, by Harold Kelman, M.D. Reprinted by permission of Science House, New York, 1971.

"Authentic Feminine Response," by Natalie Shainess, M.D., in *Sexual Behavior: Pharmacology and Biochemistry*, Raven Press, New York, 1975.

*The Hite Report*, by Shere Hite, copyright © 1976 by Shere Hite. Reprinted by permission of Macmillan Publishing Co., Inc.

"Interview with Saul Bellow," 1976. Reprinted by permission of *Time* magazine.

*Sexual Behavior in the Human Male*, by Alfred C. Kinsey, Wardell B. Pomeroy, and Clyde E. Martin. (W.B. Saunders, 1948) Institute for Sex Research.

Feature column on the Hite Report by Gerald Nachman. Reprinted by permission of the author and the author's agents, Scott Meredith Literary Agency, Inc., 845 Third Avenue, New York, New York 10022.

"Treating Goal-directed Intimacy," by Richard L. Timmers, Lloyd G. Sinclair, and Jane Rea James. Copyright 1976, National Association of Social Workers, Inc. Reprinted with permission, from *Social Work*, Vol. 21, No. 5 (September 1976), pp. 401–402.

Quotation from review by Hilton Kramer. Copyright © 1978 by The New York Times Company. Reprinted by permission.

*The Prisoner of Sex*, by Norman Mailer, Little, Brown and Co., 1971. Used by permission of the author and the author's agents, Scott Meredith Literary Agency, Inc., 845 Third Avenue, New York, New York 10022.

"Why Do These Men Hate Women," by Vivian Gornick. Reprinted by permission of *The Village Voice*. Copyright © The Village Voice, Inc., 1976.

*2000-Year-Old Misunderstanding: Rape Fantasy*, by Molly Haskell. Copyright © 1976 by Molly Haskell. Used with permission of the author.

*Eros and Ethos: A Comparative Study of Catholic, Jewish and Protestant Sex Behavior*
by Enrique Hank Lopez
Copyright © 1979 by Enrique Hank Lopez
All rights reserved. No part of this book may be reproduced in any form or by any means, except for the inclusion of brief quotations in a review, without permission in writing from the publisher. Printed in the United States of America. Prentice-Hall International, Inc., London; Prentice-Hall of Australia, Pty. Ltd., Sydney; Prentice-Hall of Canada, Ltd., Toronto; Prentice-Hall of India Private Ltd., New Delhi; Prentice-Hall of Japan, Inc., Tokyo; Prentice-Hall of Southeast Asia Pte. Ltd., Singapore; Whitehall Books Limited, Wellington, New Zealand.
10  9  8  7  6  5  4  3  2  1

**Library of Congress Cataloging in Publication Data**
Lopez, Enrique Hank.
Eros and ethos.
1.  Sex customs—United States.  2.  Catholics—
United States.  3.  Protestants—United States.
4.  Jews—United States.  I.  Title.
HQ18.U5L67    301.41'7973    78-24192
ISBN 0-13-283432-4

# Foreword by David Landy

Every ethnologist engaged in his or her initial field experience soon learns that two aspects of life in any society are more closed to outsiders than any others: sex and money. Both are fraught with strong feelings embedded in a matrix of pain and pleasure, shame and guilt, public prohibitions and private inhibitions. No other sectors of human behavior are so hedged in with secretiveness, curiosity, envy, greed, lust, affection, fear, anger, attraction and repulsion. In various societies sex may be more venerated than wealth, or vice versa, but in both of these areas of human existence the anthropologist knows that the data are likely to be least complete and probably least reliable. No matter how subtly one attempts to probe the sex or economic life of an informant, the investigator soon discovers that the subject's guard is raised and that what emerges becomes strained and disfigured through a screen of protectiveness that includes distortion, deceit and denial.

All the more remarkable, then, that the author of this book was able to elicit such free and candid discussions from his informants. They seem to respond with surprising frankness and honesty, opening up their wounds of pride and longing, displaying their frailties and confusions with a candor that is granted only the most skillful interviewer. Even more amazing is Enrique Lopez' feat of personally interviewing all 722 of his subjects! I know of no parallel in the behavioral sciences. It assures, as Lopez notes, that at the very least, interviewer bias is held constant.

One of the more tantalizing discoveries in the book is that a macho attitude toward sex, and presumably toward other aspects of life (most especially toward women), seems to be associated with religious orthodoxy. While this does not necessarily in itself constitute news, it begs for further research to determine the social and cultural correlates of this linkage.

What features of religious fundamentalism constrain toward both a sharp distinction in sex roles and a push toward male braggadocio regarding sexual prowess? Are such behaviors and attitudes really an expression of one's position in a particular kind of social structure with sexual behavior an incidental rather than determining factor?

Lopez casts an appreciative but skeptical eye in Freud's direction, suggesting that a stronger case might be made for the development priority of breast envy over penis envy, in both sexes, and his data seem to support him. While many readers will seize on this notion as having at least face plausibility, if not validity, an anthropologist must caution that the finding may be an artifact of psychosexual development in the culture of the United States. Crosscultural evidence points to many societies in which the female breast receives far less veneration, exploitation or attraction in sexual display and behavior. Internal evidence in the present study also points in this direction, for example, the finding that there are "no discernible differences between Jewish and gentile children with respect to their early sexual behavior and attitudes" until adolescence. Lopez' study also opens up the Freudian concept of the Oedipal conflict by suggesting that the male child's envy and resentment of the father "is not sexual but merely nutritional" when the infant boy is deprived of his mother's breast.

The book tells us that the Jewish American Princess stereotype (the notion of the Jewish female as something very special, spoiled, willful, domineering) has its complement in the Jewish American Prince. But it is hinted that counterparts also exist in other groups, especially Catholics, which raises in my mind the possibility that the syndrome may derive more from life in middle-class United States society than from membership in any particular religious or ethnic segment of that society. And the Jewish male *shiksa* complex, the longing for a woman representing the stereotyped and mythical cynosure of the dominant ethnic group, surely finds its equal in other ethnic minorities, as Lopez' material also suggests.

The similarities among these religious and ethnic groupings seem to be as prevalent as the differences, perhaps more so, indicating again the possibly homogenizing effects of American culture. One might predict that in another genera-

tion, cross-ethnic and cross-religious differences will be further
thinned out, perhaps even washed away. Social class may be a
more powerful differentiator than subculture or religion, as
certain occupational differences in this study suggest.

While members of all three religions seem to be moving
toward more "liberated" sexual behavior, one also perceives
that the ancient double-standard, especially on the part of
American males, tends to persist. If this proves out in the larger
society, the widening disparity between freer attitudes toward
sex on the one hand, and the strain against a single standard on
the other may generate greater rather than lesser sexual conflict than in past generations.

In their groundbreaking study of sexual behavior across
cultures and across mammalian species of three decades ago,
Clellan S. Ford and Frank A. Beach refer in their conclusions to
their "appreciation of the necessity of viewing sexual behavior
in broad perspective, and of interpreting the habits of any particular group of human beings in terms of the broad background provided by the cross-cultural and cross-species evidence." They go on to point out how critical it is to use such a
framework in approaching the study of sexual behavior in
American life. While they refer to the work of Kinsey as more
or less representing patterns of sexual behavior in the United
States, they did not have available research on cross-ethnic patterns within our larger society. Enrique Lopez' book is both
cross-ethnic and cross-religious, and it is, as far as I know, the
first systematic attempt to be so in regard to sexual behavior.

Behavioral scientists will wish for more specifics on the
methodology of the study, and especially on the nature of the
sampling techniques. Some will long for the conventional ac-
coutrements of probability statistics and computer runs, and
bemoan the absence of footnotes and other embellishments of
the social science monograph. But Lopez has rather a different
aim here. He is addressing not a closed company of scientific
colleagues, but the general reader, and his first aim is to com-
municate directly and quickly his findings, deductions and in-
ferences without burdening his material with the ponderous
paraphernalia of the professional. Even so, while the book will
fascinate, inform and amuse the lay person, it will be of keen
interest to social scientists who could profitably take off from

any of the dozens of leads and insights that mark the work. They, too, will be fascinated, informed and amused.

Half a century ago Bronislaw Malinowski wrote what is still the finest study of sexual behavior in a preindustrial society, based upon his superb field work among the Trobriand Islanders, *The Sexual Life of Savages*. In it he said, "Sex, in its widest meaning—and it is thus I have used it in the title of this book—is rather a sociological and cultural force than a mere bodily relation of two individuals. . . . The anthropologist must therefore give a description of the direct approaches of the two lovers, . . . shaped by their traditions, obeying their laws, following the customs of their tribe." The reader will glimpse, in the present volume, a rich if yet incomplete portrayal of the sexual life of his or her friends and neighbors "following the customs of their tribe."

—Dr. David Landy
Professor of Cultural Anthropology
University of Massachusetts

(Author of *Culture, Disease and Healing*)

# Preface

Several years ago, while teaching as a Regents Professor at the University of California, I participated in a seminar on "Machismo as a Universal Trait," during which I became firmly convinced that ethnic environments play a dominant role in the sexual development of all human beings.

Indeed, upon rereading Freud, I could easily discern how his Jewish upbringing had deeply influenced his most basic theories, particularly those relating to sex. Acutely aware of the machismo in my own Mexican environment, I detected numerous traces of similar yet somehow different macho attitudes in Freud's behavior. During subsequent discussions of this phenomenon with three colleagues, one of them suggested that I make a comparative study of the sexual behavior of various ethnic groups, stressing the influence of religious and cultural pressures on specific individuals within each group.

Having occasionally wondered about the sociocultural basis of my own erotic behavior, I needed only minimal encouragement. Consequently, I soon thereafter launched what was to become a six-year study involving 722 interviews with persons of three religious backgrounds—Catholic, Protestant and Jewish. But within a few months I realized that Jewish men and women were far more willing to discuss their sexual behavior than either Catholics or Protestants. When I mentioned this to a Jewish colleague, she immediately suggested that I focus on Jewish sexual mores as compared with a more limited sample of gentiles.

"But that's your province," I said. "It may be," she answered, "but I might not have the objectivity you might have. And besides, your Mexican machismo would give you a certain kinship and a special insight into our kind of machismo. Yet you would be less emotionally involved than any of us, less apt to skew your findings to fit prior assumptions or prejudices."

Though tempted by her suggestion, I ultimately decided to pursue my original "tri-ethos" approach, thereafter interviewing 239 Catholics, 241 Protestants and 242 Jews. The basis of these interviews was a four-page questionnaire which I prepared with the advice of two colleagues—a sociologist and a psychologist. My own Catholic upbringing gave me some insight into the sexual attitudes of my Catholic interviewees, but to sharpen my perceptions of the Jewish ethos, I attended several different types of religious rites: a circumcision ceremony, called a *bris*; two *Bar mitzvahs*, one Reform and the other Orthodox; a very formal Orthodox wedding; a *Bas mitzvah* for seven 13-year-old girls; two very solemn services during Rosh Hashana and Yom Kippur; and several regular Saturday-morning services in temples representing varying degrees of tradition and modernism.

Having thus been exposed to the religious aspect of Jewish culture, I was all the more convinced that one cannot adequately understand the sexual attitudes and practices of most Jews without some prior knowledge of their religion or lack of same. For example, one can more than likely predict the degree of machismo in a man's makeup by the degree of orthodoxy in his religion—the more orthodox, the more macho—as will be seen in chapter 3. Similarly, the male Jew's attitude toward supposedly forbidden gentile women (*shiksas*) can also be traced, directly or indirectly, to some religious and/or cultural source.

In this respect, it is interesting to note that several interviewees (both men and women) seemed to "feel more Jewish" when dating or having affairs with gentiles than when they dated or had affairs with fellow Jews. This eventually prompted me to interview seventy-five gentile women and seventy-five gentile men who had experienced sexual relations with Jews, hoping to determine how they felt about such interethnic sex. Their answers were extremely significant, though often complex and contradictory (see chapter 10); but one recurrent finding that merits special attention is that these particular gentile women have a higher regard for Jewish men than do Jewish women. Gentile men, on the other hand, are often overwhelmed by Jewish women, particularly if such men are WASPs from the Middle West. For example, a very solemn-mannered

dentist from Iowa told us that "Jewish women are too intellectual and too darned candid about sex, and some of them seem
to be making fun of sex—even at the most serious stage."

As one might expect, the data indicate measurable differences in the sexual attitudes of Irish Catholics and *Latino*
Catholics; and there were also differences between Jews of different national origins—that is, between Russian Jews and
German Jews, Spanish Jews and Polish Jews, and so on. (Russian Jews, for example, seem to be more creative sex partners
than German Jews.) In fact, one of my interviewees, a young
mathematician from an Ivy League college, has devised a
rather complex theorem which presumably predicts the "virility
quotient" of different types of Jewish lovers in various erotic
settings—such as the "VQ" of a married Polish Jew committing
adultery with a gentile divorcée who is a lapsed Catholic and a
mother of two teenaged girls. His unique and intellectually
challenging "VQ Equation" appears in chapter 5, with appro-
priate illustrations.

While on the subject of virility, one should note that
Jewish men and women apparently have a longer span of sexual activity than Catholics and Protestants—an average of three
or four years longer—even though Jews seem to experience a
wider variety of psychological hang-ups. Judging from the
composite data of the 722 interviews, as compared with data
from other studies, Jews over fifty years of age are more sexually active and virile than WASPs in the same age bracket.
(Supporting statistics and analysis appear in chapter 7.) Their
sexual longevity, according to one psychologist, may be attributed to experimental attitudes or "more sybaritic life-styles."
Needless to say, the interviewees' candid revelations lend themselves to various other speculations, some of which are distinctly
non-Freudian.

Not surprisingly, their sexual profiles vary according to
their respective occupations. The more cerebral professionals
(lawyers, doctors, professors, psychologists) are apt to engage in
extended and varied foreplay, but their "staying power" in actual intercourse tends to be limited and sporadic; whereas less-
educated cabdrivers, waiters, plant employees and union organizers are apt to shun foreplay but have greater staying
power in what is usually very conventional fornication. Similar

occupational differences appear in the sexual attitudes and practices of women, though women are generally more experimental than their male counterparts. Such differences are easily discerned in the data gathered from the 722 interviewees, among whom were 4 lawyers, 2 dentists, 12 teachers, 5 cabdrivers, 3 waitresses, 2 waiters, 2 psychologists, 1 mortician, 1 stockbroker, 2 union organizers, 16 secretaries, 2 farmers, 71 housewives, 1 sex therapist, 2 insurance men, 17 plant employees, 1 politician, 2 social workers, 2 electricians, 3 professors, 2 accountants, 13 salesmen, 3 doctors, 4 nurses, 1 hotel manager, 2 hotel employees, 1 masseuse, 2 druggists, 2 plumbers, 2 actors, 1 barber, 1 writer, 1 printer, 1 television repairman, 23 students, 1 prostitute, 2 unemployed hospital workers and representatives of a wide variety of other occupations.

Aside from *vocational* differences in sexual attitudes and practices, there are certain remarkable differences between men and women. With respect to oral sex, for example, there are fewer men willing to engage in cunnilingus than women willing to engage in fellatio, the reasons for which are set forth and analyzed in chapter 9.

Such male-female divergences occur in both gentile and Jewish groups; but there are, nonetheless, certain sexual behavior patterns that are definitely related to ethnic and cultural factors, as will be seen in various phases of this survey. Although these interviewees may not necessarily represent a true cross section of the various ethnic groups in America (no survey can ever achieve that cherished goal), they are sufficiently diverse to give us some valuable insights and considerable information about race, religion and sex.

—Enrique Lopez

# Contents

# Note on Interviewing Technique

Since I personally interviewed every one of the 722 men and women involved in this survey, the readers of this text are entitled to know about my training and experience as an interviewer and researcher. Here, then, is a brief résumé of my personal involvement in matters directly or indirectly related to this particular study.

My first major experience as an interviewer occurred while I was attending Harvard University, first as a graduate student of economics and then as a student and subsequent graduate of the Harvard Law School. During my initial period in Cambridge I lived in a commune of graduate students, most of whom were doctoral candidates in psychology; it was through this happenstance that I worked for two years as a psychiatric interviewer in an experiment jointly conducted by the Harvard Medical School's Department of Psychiatry and the psychiatric division of the Massachusetts General Hospital. A visitor at our commune, having heard that I had been a Gallup Poll interviewer and a Spanish-to-English interpreter for psychiatrists in a U.S. Army hospital, apparently assumed that I was a doctoral student in psychology and recommended me as a replacement for the psychiatric interviewer who was leaving the aforementioned experiment. The man I replaced was Dr. Paul Gebhardt, who become Dr. Alfred Kinsey's junior colleague in the soon-to-be famous Kinsey report on the sexual behavior of American men and women. Dr. Gebhardt is now director of the Kinsey Institute for Sexual Research.

My second major experience as an interviewer occurred in 1953–54, when I interviewed 200 Mexican men and women for a projected doctoral thesis on "The Psycho-Social Basis of Machismo." I had taken a sabbatical leave from my law practice in California to study for a Ph.D. in psychology at the Univer-

sidad Nacional Antonoma de Mexico and I had nearly com-
pleted the required courses; but the chairman of my doctoral
committee was so incensed by what he called "the obscene
anti-Mexican bias" of my thesis that he refused to approve it.
Indeed, he grabbed the first draft of my manuscript and tossed
it out of a tenth-story window into a torrential rain—all of
which permanently dampened my enthusiasm for that particular project.

My subsequent experience as an interviewer and re-
searcher included a six-week tape-recorded interview with
Lyndon Johnson's brother, Sam Houston Johnson, which was
later converted into a jointly authored book titled *My Brother
Lyndon*. Thereafter I conducted a four-week interview with
Vital Alsar for a book titled *La Balsa*.

I should also mention that my twelve years' experience as
a trial lawyer, conducting countless direct and cross-exam-
inations, required many of the same techniques that enabled
me to conduct in-depth interviews with the aforementioned
722 persons who, at first reluctantly, then quite willingly, revealed the most intimate details of their sexual behavior.

Most of the interviews were at least four hours long and
each of them covered all of the questions in a carefully prepared questionnaire. However, the interviewees were permitted to wander or diverge from any particular question so as to
provide for a maximum of ease and candor.

Moreover, in order to minimize what might be called "the
interviewer variable," which inevitably results when different
interviewers ask the same question in different ways, I decided
from the very outset to conduct all of the interviews myself.
This has not necessarily eliminated interviewer bias, but at least
the bias is uniform.

Freud also embodies two traditions almost as antithetical as romanticism and nineteenth-century scientism. He was profoundly a Jew, not in a doctrinal sense but in his conception of morality, in his love of the skeptical play of reason, in his distrust of illusion, in the form of his prophetic talent, even in his conception of mature eroticism. Wisdom for Freud was neither doctrine nor formula but the achievement of maturity. The patient who is cured is the one who is free enough of neurosis to decide intelligently about his own identity. As for his conception of mature love, it has always seemed to me that its blend of tenderness and sensuality combined the uxorious imagery of the Hasidic tradition and the sensual quality of the Song of Songs. And might it not have been Freud rather than a commentator of the Haftorahs who said, "In children, it was taught, God gives humanity a chance to make good its mistakes"?

—Jerome S. Bruner, *On Knowing*

# 1
# Early Sexual Development

## PENIS ENVY VERSUS BREAST ENVY_____

As Sigmund Freud so persuasively theorized, most of our lifelong sexual behavior and attitudes are deeply influenced by experiences in our infancy and early childhood. Indeed, it was Freud's Judaeo-macho childhood environment which led him to the supramasculine assumption that the male sex organ is of prime importance, which in turn led him to the corollary assumption that most females suffer from *penis envy*. But judging from data obtained from our 722 in-depth interviews, we may well wonder why Freud failed to explore the more likely hypothesis that most males suffer from *breast envy*.

Anyone sufficiently free of Freudian bias, who has indeed observed infants in their most formative stages, will readily acknowledge that a child's first and primary concern is his or her mother's breasts. It is not until much later that the child concerns himself or herself with the presence or absence of a penis. By then, of course, the child's often obsessive attachment to his or her mother's breasts has become a dominant and durable fixture in his developing psyche. Not only have the mother's breasts provided the only physical sustenance in the early months of infancy, but they have also become a psychic need— an indispensable source of emotional comfort. Indeed, as one considers the soft, pliable warmth of the mother's breasts, one is tempted to hypothesize that a child's (or any adult's) subsequent need for a pillow is directly related to that early nestling against a maternal bosom.

Although most people have only vague memories of their childhood concerns and anxieties, about 70 percent of my male interviewees distinctly remembered having some degree of concern about not having breasts like their mothers', whereas

1

only 60 percent of the female interviewees remembered having some degree of penis envy. Moreover, 50 percent of these females recalled having some degree of breast envy, which of course later disappeared when they themselves began developing breasts. A random sample of their comments will suffice to illustrate this childhood obsession with the maternal bosom.

> *Male:* "I used to stare at myself in the mirror, standing sideways sometimes, wondering when I would have breasts like my mother's."
>
> *Male:* "I often asked my mother when I would get big like her, and she would just laugh at me."
>
> *Female:* "When I was only four years old, I would wrap my mother's bra around my puny chest and pretend I had big tits."
>
> *Male:* "I remember trying to wear my mother's brassiere and my dad getting mad at me and pulling my ear."
>
> *Female:* "My mother kept promising me I'd be like her, and I kept staring at the mirror day after day, wondering when it would happen."
>
> *Male:* "One night when my dad and I were pissing together, he shook his penis and said, 'This is what we got that your mom and sister ain't got.' And I remember saying, 'But mommy is bigger up here,' which made him sort of angry at me."
>
> *Female:* "Sure, I remember wanting a penis like my brother, but I also wanted breasts like my mother had."
>
> *Male:* "I wanted a bigger penis like my dad, but I guess I also wanted boobs like my mother—big ones."
>
> *Female:* "I used to pinch and pull at my chest to make myself grow breasts like my mother and Aunt Tilly."

With respect to this last comment, one should note that a careful observation of any child between three and five years old will reveal an occasional tendency to pinch or massage his/her chest as if to force the growth of breasts. Moreover, this obsession with mammary development generally occurs *before* such children become interested in the penis phenomenon, which Freud erroneously regarded as the first anatomical concern of young children.

Considering the importance thus attributed to the mother's breasts, one must expect that the child will eventually notice an absence of breasts in himself or herself and that she or he will feel grossly deficient in this respect.

Consequently, although one might concede that Freud was correct in assuming that most young girls develop penis envy, one must stress the fact that all children (both female and male) suffer from an acute breast envy that precedes, supersedes and greatly overshadows any degree of penis envy. Freud himself (had he not been distracted by his own macho propensities) should have recognized this alternative hypothesis when one of his own patients described his penis as "an extended nipple," or when another patient complained that "my testicles feel like puny little breasts that have been misplaced." Given Freud's proverbial reputation for imaginative analogies, one may well wonder what personal repressions caused him to desist from pursuing such obvious clues to their logical conclusion.

Assuming, then (as I think we must), that breast envy plays a crucial role in the development of the human psyche, one must then re-explore and reappraise the Oedipus complex as it relates to this initial obsession. First of all, let us consider the male infant. From the very first day of his infancy—indeed, within a few short hours of his birth—he develops an overwhelmingly irresistible attachment to his mother's breasts. Whenever he feels the onset of hunger or fear or a sudden sense of abandonment, he cries for his mother; and when she picks him up he immediately reaches for her bosom as if some primitive instinct guides him in that direction. And as he suckles her teat he feels the comforting warmth, softness and pliability of her breast, so that he inevitably associates all these factors with an instant satisfaction of several often indefinable needs.

Later, after he has been weaned from breast feeding (much against his own wishes) and begins to compare his own body with those around him, he becomes acutely aware of the fact that he lacks the abundant breasts his mother has. He also realizes that his father lacks breasts and is therefore deficient in a most basic sense. Freud would have us believe that during this period, the young male child has developed a certain pride in having a penis and that his sister or female playmates have become envious of his little appendage. But isn't it more logical to assume that he considers his penis a poor substitute for breasts? As a matter of fact, his penis is often a source of annoyance and embarrassment. Witness, for example, these childhood memories:

"It was always my penis that kept wetting my pants and making my parents mad at me."

"My schoolmates used to tease me for wetting my pants, which made me resent my penis for causing all the trouble."

"My penis itched a lot, so I had to scratch it, and my dad bawled me out in front of everybody."

"Whenever I played with myself—sometimes not even thinking about it—my old man said it would stunt my growth."

The threat of stunted growth seems universal. When I was four years old, for example, I went to a carnival where my godfather pointed to a dwarf and solemnly told me, *"Es lo que pasa cuando juegas con tu verga"*—"That's what happens when you play with your prick." It was such a frightening prospect that for two weeks I absolutely refused to touch my penis—even when urinating; I simply let the urine flow anywhere it chose to go, generally wetting my pants and messing the bathroom floor. At that particular stage of my life (and I am sure my reactions were not much different from those of my peers) Dr. Freud would have had considerable difficulty convincing me that I was better endowed than my female cousins—this despite the occasional erotic pleasure I got from furtive masturbation.

As for erotic satisfaction, one must bear in mind the oral pleasure that all children experience from breast or bottle feeding. For most people, the need for oral eroticism is a lifelong phenomenon. When in subsequent years the male nibbles and sucks on the nipples of his female lover, he would prefer to think that he is merely complying with the female's need for sexual foreplay, when in fact he may be regressing to a long-repressed infantile attachment to his mother. By the same reasoning, one might conclude that fellatio is an adult female's return to the maternal breast, although conventional Freudians might argue for an intertwined paternal-maternal fixation.

*Incidentally, as far as I am able to ascertain from my composite interview data, there are no discernible differences between Jewish and gentile children with respect to their early sexual behavior and attitudes, although there are certain marked differences at a later stage.*

Going back to the male child's attachment to the maternal breasts, the interviewees' comments indicate that, far from resenting his father as a rival for his mother's affection, the small boy may actually disdain his father for having a flat chest and thus may see him as weak, useless and deformed. Should he happen to see his parents in precoital foreplay, with his father kissing and fondling the mother's breasts, the child more than likely regards his father as a *fellow infant* encroaching on his terrain—so that his envy is not sexual but merely nutritional. The following remarks from some male respondents would seem to substantiate this hypothesis:

"I remember thinking that my dad was taking my milk, even though I was four years old and had been weaned long ago. I even tried to push him away so I could suck her breasts again, and they both laughed at me."

"I saw him sucking her breasts and I remember hating him—really hating him."

"My dad used to suck her breasts all the time. I started noticing this when I was three or four years old, and I felt like I was being cheated from something that was really mine."

"He looked like a goddamned baby sucking her tits that way."

"Look, I don't want to talk about my dad sucking her breasts. It really makes me sick to think about it, if you want to know the truth."

Having thus seen his father as a rival overgrown infant forever competing for possession of the wife-mother's breasts, the child's initial envy soon develops into outright hatred, which may or may not remain quiescent, depending upon his response to the societal pressures that impinge upon all human emotions. But even in those cases where the child-boy-man or child-girl-woman has successfully resolved the so-called Oedipus or Electra conflict, there is always a residue of that childhood envy and resentment, some of which surfaces at odd times and odd places. Take, for example, the following recollections gleaned from some of my interviews:

Male: "I guess I hated my dad until I was out of high school, but I could never figure out *why* I hated him. He was really a pretty nice guy, a helluva lot better than most of the fathers in our neighborhood, but I still resented him."

*Male:* "My mom kept telling me not to hate him, that he was really okay, but I just couldn't stand him—at least not until I got older."

*Female:* "I thought my mom was a real bitch (maybe I still do), but my dad was really super. And he was better-looking than any guy around."

*Female:* "My mother was always trying to come between me and my dad. I mean she really resented it when he would take me to the ball games at Fenway Park. She was so damned jealous."

*Male:* "Like I really didn't think my dad was good enough for my mother. It wasn't until later on that I had any respect for him."

*Female:* "I kept having this dream that my mother had died and I had married my dad, and it made me feel guilty as hell, but I kept dreaming the same damned dream. After a while, I couldn't look her in the eye."

More than 84 percent of the women admitted, some more freely than others, that they had once hated or resented their mothers. Their feelings ranged from bitter hatred to mere disdain ("She was so stupid" . . . "Just a kvetch"), but such feelings either diminish or are simply repressed at a later age. As for the men I interviewed, about 70 percent were willing to admit they had once hated their fathers, but I believe that percentage would be higher if some of those who denied such hatred had been more candid. And many of those who did acknowledge such feelings were quick to add remarks such as, "Now this wasn't because I had some sort of crush on my mother; it's just that my old man was such a bastard." Interestingly enough, gentile males are more apt to hate their fathers than are Jewish males; whereas Jewish females seem to resent their mothers more than do gentile females. Whether this is true in early childhood would be difficult to ascertain, since inward emotions are generally more difficult to remember than certain specific physical activities.

For example, more than 90 percent of the male interviewees clearly remembered masturbating during early childhood, about 40 percent doing so on a fairly regular basis through their early teens. About 42 percent of the females engaged in masturbation in pre-adolescence, and an additional 34 percent admitted "exploring" or fingering their vaginal or clitoral areas without actually masturbating. The data also indicate that masturbation is an exceedingly private activity for young girls, seldom if ever done in the presence of anyone else. But for many boys it is often a social activity, with two or more youngsters openly participating in what might be called a genital jam session. One interviewee laughingly recalled a game that was played in his neighborhood near Forest Hills. "We used to stand in a circle and jerk off, and the last kid to get a hard-on was the loser; so then everyone else would spit on his penis. It was really a great game, but we stopped playing it when we got to junior high school." Smiling as he fondly recalled those early tests of masculinity, he proudly asserted that he had never finished last. "I was a real fast jerker in those days, so I never got spit on."

Though none of the women could recall any comparable tests of femininity, at least 62 percent remembered participating in the time-honored game of "Let's play doctor," some of them wryly commenting, "We girls were always the patient but never the doctor." Since 76 percent of the males had once been little doctors, whose only specialty was genital examinations, one can only assume that there were more doctors than patients, which means that certain patients were attended by more than one doctor. In fact, one of my female interviewees, a psychologist, distinctly recalled a rainy Sunday afternoon "when I was closely examined by seven very curious eight-year-old doctors, three of whom subsequently allowed me to play nurse so that I could examine their very interesting but rather puny and ticklish genitals."

Occasionally there have been serious deviations from normal little-boy curiosity, as revealed by the following:

"My father used to play 'doctor' with me when I was about five or six years old, and it wasn't until much later that I realized he was just a dirty old man."

"I guess it was my slightly older brother who played the 'little doctor' game with me. He was always pulling down my pants and examining my crotch with one of those pencil flashlights."

"When I was five or six years old, I had this twenty-year-old uncle (my mother's older brother) who was always pretending to be the doctor. He would take me and my sister to the game room in the basement, where he said it was easier to make a good examination."

Most of the interviewees remembered participating in more innocent pastimes, such as spin-the-bottle and other kissing games. About 40 percent of the females played these games from the ages of ten to twelve, and the percentage rose an additional 30 points from the ages of thirteen to fourteen. Most boys began these games at twelve years of age, with less than 50 percent participating on any regular basis. "Boys were always shy at that age," observed one woman. "They didn't like to kiss as much as we did, but you could always get them to wrestle, which was really sexier than just plain kissing—unless it was French kissing, which hardly any boy liked."

## INCIPIENT HOMOSEXUALITY

Yielding to social pressures in their prepuberty years, boys generally tend to avoid girls and concentrate their plentiful energies on athletic activities. And with all the close and continuous bodily contact in exclusively masculine settings, certain incipient homosexual tendencies are bound to surface. As Alfred C. Kinsey observed many years ago, "The anatomy and functional capacities of male genitalia interest the younger boy to a degree that is not appreciated by older males who have become heterosexually conditioned and who are continuously on the defensive against reactions which might be interpreted as homosexual."

In the present survey, about 54 percent of the adult males recalled participating in some form of boy-with-boy sexual activity, usually at the age of nine or ten; but I suspect that percentage may be a little low. Thirty years ago, in more restrictive times, Kinsey reported that "about half of the older males (48%) and nearly two-thirds (60%) of the boys who were preadolescent at the time they contributed their histories, recall homosexual activity in their pre-adolescent years." Only 10 percent of the Jewish males refused to talk about homosexuality, as compared with 28 percent of the WASPs. Yet among those who freely discussed the subject, the percentage of young boys engaging in homosexual play was about the same for Jews and gentiles. Gentile women, however, seemed almost as uninhibited as Jewish women in discussing homosexuality, with only 8 percent and 6 percent of the respective groups refusing to offer any comment, which is not to say that they all admitted to some degree of homosexual play in their early childhood. Nevertheless, about 65 percent reported at least minimal participation, much of which was more emotional than physical:

"I had a real crush on this girl in my Scout troop, but I would have been afraid to touch her. So all I did was just stare at her and feel my temple throbbing. Eventually, I married her brother."

"That was a terrible time for me. I had this awful crush on my friend Julie, and we used to trade skirts and sweaters all the time—but if she ever wore another girl's skirt, I would just die of jealousy."

"This friend and I used to walk around holding hands all the time and one night I slept over at her house and we took a shower together and she started tickling my you-know-what. I guess it felt good, but I suddenly jumped out of the shower and nearly cracked my knee. So we never showered together again, and after a while she wouldn't hold hands any more."

Although generally less direct, boys sometimes develop equally intense crushes that are sometimes masked with roughhouse play:

"All of a sudden I started feeling this crazy damn thing whenever our shortstop started rassling with me and grabbing my crotch, which he did to all the guys. Well, I didn't know how they felt, but it made my heart thump and I would shake all over."

"Ron and I used to go fishing at this reservoir and we'd spend the night in the tent, snuggled together to keep warm. But I could never sleep because I kept wanting to kiss him somewhere. I still get this funny feeling that I'm liable to kiss him—and, Jesus Christ, we're both married and have grown kids!"

"Someone was always grabbing at your prick when you took showers at school."

## ADOLESCENT SEX BEHAVIOR

It is during adolescence that Catholics, Jews and Protestants begin to differ with respect to their sexual attitudes and behavior. First of all, Jews are more verbal than gentiles and are thus likely to talk more freely about a wider range of subjects, including sex. One might attribute this verbal aptitude to the fact that most Jews live in large urban centers and city people generally talk more than small-town or rural people, and this may be partially true; but even within the major metropolitan areas, Jews have a higher verbal output than other groups. Consequently, they talk more about sex, because sex is one of the more fascinating aspects of everyday conversation

Moreover, Jews have a high degree of skepticism and inquisitiveness, often, for example, making statements in the form of rhetorical questions, as if questioning their own assertions. Jewish adolescents on the verge of engaging in sex are thus apt to get involved in endless discussions about the whys and wherefores of sexual involvement. At least 65 percent of my Jewish interviewees, both female and male, clearly remember these "very heavy" discussions, many of which eventually nullified the intended sexual enterprise. One of the men, a middle-aged dentist from Los Angeles, wryly commented: "My girl and I would talk about it so goddamned much—I mean from every angle—that I would lose my hard-on. I knew she was a virgin because she was such a good talker." Adding substance to that notion, one female respondent told me that her mother always advised her to "just keep talking, Shirley, and he'll never lay you—he'll eventually give up. And besides, when you're talking he can't French kiss you, which is where all the trouble starts."

Several examples of these erotic-but-evasive conversations occur in the film *Bananas*, in which Woody Allen and Louise Lasser constantly talk themselves into a sexual impasse. Their humorously soulful discussions also point up the fact that Jews are more apt to joke about sex and love than Catholics or Protestants are, particularly non-Latin, white gentiles. This penchant for poking fun at sex, which some people consider deadly serious business, will occasionally puzzle and irritate an adolescent gentile male earnestly wooing an outwardly sexy Jewish girl. One would-be lover subsequently told me about his frustrations: "This girl Rhoda would always get me hot and bothered, like my nuts were ready to pop, then suddenly she'd start getting clever and cute. She'd even make jokes about my erection, till I'd finally come in her hand or just go limp like a soft banana. Then I'd go find myself one of those Italian or Irish girls at our high school, maybe not as smart as Rhoda, but at least ready to screw without any wisecracks."

At least 40 percent of the gentile interviewees recalled

similarly frustrating experiences, and 62 percent of the Jewish male interviewees reported the same frustrations in adolescence—but most of them said they had fully expected such ploys and rather enjoyed the give-and-take humor involved therein. "If you can't have an orgasm, at least you can get a good laugh," one of them told me with a casual shrug.

Referring to such erotic humor, a Catholic priest once speculated that "most jokes about sex are probably invented by Jewish comedians." His reasoning was based on the undoubted fact that at least 80 percent of the most successful nightclub comedians are Jewish, and that most nightclub humor is related to sex. Several months later, I attended two shows in Las Vegas and studiously counted and classified all the jokes I heard; exactly 70 percent in one show and 85 percent in the other concerned sex. The 70 percent were told by a Jewish comedian, and the 85 percent by an Italian—which might indicate that sex humor is the product of occupation rather than ethnic origin. But since most good humor (about sex or any other subject) is based on irony, one could just as easily argue that Jews are more humorous because their ethos is so full of skepticism and inquisitiveness.

Perhaps it is these two qualities that attract so many Jews into the fields of psychology, psychiatry and psychoanalysis, most of which are dominated by Jewish men. Moreover, since sex is of prime concern in all these disciplines, perhaps their professional preference points to a personal obsession with sex. Indeed, a graduate student in psychology at Harvard used to tell his friends that he'd gotten into the field because of all the wet dreams he had been having since the age of thirteen, commencing with his Bar Mitzvah. "I still have wet dreams," he would add, "but now I know why I have them."

A fellow doctoral candidate had been obsessed with gentile girls during his adolescence. "Shiksas were forbidden fruit," he once told me, "and that's what made them doubly attractive to some of us. They were also supposed to be easier to screw than most Jewish girls. Consequently, I used to have these fantasies of screwing every shiksa in our high-school pep club, all those button-nosed blondes. But all I could do was fantasize in those days—fantasize and jerk off once in a while—yet I was never able to make it with anyone, gentile or Jew."

In this respect, he sounds like Portnoy, the famous protagonist of Philip Roth's controversial novel. One should note that this particular attitude is not uncommon. About 25 percent of my interviewees reported similar yearnings for shiksas, some merely fantasizing and others (about 70 percent of that 25 percent) successfully carrying out their fantasies with actual intercourse. Mexicans in Mexico and Chicanos in this country have a comparable obsession with so-called *gringas*—that is, Caucasian females from the U.S. Perhaps unconsciously disdaining their own Indian or *mestizo* brown skin, they seem to prefer lighter skin and blonde hair, which many of my fellow Mexicans will hotly deny. Some, in fact, will insist that the only reason they pursue gringas is that they are supposedly easier to seduce. And it's probably true that Mexican and Chicano girls are less likely to engage in premarital sex, a reticence that reflects the virginity complex that is literally forced upon them by Mexican machos who demand that their prospective brides remain virgins until the wedding night. Given this obsession with virginity and its corollary, the virgin-mother complex, it is not too surprising that many Mexicans stop having intercourse with their wives when they become mothers, or at least greatly reduce such activity. Machismo, then, may be nothing more than a disguised mother fixation, since a macho may consider relations with his wife-become-mother as symbolically incestuous; whereas a mistress presents no such taboo. In other words, mothers are not meant for sex.

This same pattern exists among Caucasian gentiles and Jews, according to my composite data. About 65 percent of the gentile wives and 60 percent of the Jewish wives sadly revealed that their marital intercourse had greatly diminished after they had become mothers. "I simply assumed that my vagina had gotten too loose," one of them said. "But my mother and older sister warned me about that. They had also warned me not to have sex before marriage with any of the Jewish boys I dated in high school, because they wouldn't marry someone who wasn't a virgin. So, in the final analysis, I didn't have many years for screwing—except for a Greek I fooled around with in my senior year of high school." (About 50 percent of the Jewish women who had resisted sex with Jewish males freely admitted having simultaneously yielded to gentile lovers at least once.)

For an opposite view of this syndrome, one should read Rhoda Lehrman's amusing novel *The Girl That He Marries*, in which a very macho Jewish protagonist lavishes his erotic energies on everyone except the sex-starved WASP he plans to marry. Her surrogate-Jewish-princess strategems for overcoming his virgin-bride complex are truly heroic and marvelously witty.

Getting back to the comparative sexual behavior of Jewish and gentile adolescents, the following statistics should be of interest:

*Masturbation*

| | |
|---|---|
| Gentile males from 14 to 18 years old | 92% |
| Jewish males from 14 to 18 years old | 90% |
| Gentile females from 14 to 18 years old | 85% |
| Jewish females from 14 to 18 years old | 90% |

*Petting to Climax*

| | |
|---|---|
| Gentile males from 14 to 18 years old | 65% |
| Jewish males from 14 to 18 years old | 80% |
| Gentile females from 14 to 18 years old | 50% |
| Jewish females from 14 to 18 years old | 80% |

NOTE: "Climax" for females usually refers to orgasm experienced by the male partner.

*Actual Intercourse*

| | |
|---|---|
| Gentile males from 14 to 18 years old | 45% |
| Jewish males from 14 to 18 years old | 48% |
| Gentile females from 14 to 18 years old | 52% |
| Jewish females from 14 to 18 years old | 22% |

*Pregnancy and Abortion*

| | |
|---|---|
| Gentile females from 14 to 18 years old | 24% |
| Jewish females from 14 to 18 years old | 14% |

*Oral Sex Other Than Petting*

| | |
|---|---|
| Gentile males from 14 to 18 years old | 8% |
| Jewish males from 14 to 18 years old | 22% |
| Gentile females from 14 to 18 years old | 25% |
| Jewish females from 14 to 18 years old | 38% |

*Homosexual Arousal and/or Orgasm*

| | |
|---|---:|
| Gentile males from 14 to 18 years old | 14% |
| Jewish males from 14 to 18 years old | 13% |
| Gentile females from 14 to 18 years old | 18% |
| Jewish females from 14 to 18 years old | 18% |

## CULTURAL INFLUENCE ON SEX BEHAVIOR_____

### The Princess Syndrome

On the cover of the September 1976 issue of *Esquire* there is an announcement for a short story by William Styron which reads: "Jewish Princess—Do Not Touch?" Judging from the data I have compiled, the announcement should have been: "Jewish Princess—Touch But Do Not Enter!"

As one can gather from the foregoing statistical profiles, Jewish adolescent females are notorious and obviously successful teasers. They are creatively talkative about sex, they can tell the latest risqué jokes with a promising come-hitherness, they often pet furiously enough to make their partners come, but very rarely do they actually go all the way. The rich spoiled Princess in Styron's story (and one suspects that he was the WASP who letched and lost) is an almost textbook example of this much-celebrated product of the Jewish ethos. The proud, doting father places her on a pedestal at a very early age, bends to her every wish and whim (if he can afford it) and has periodic nightmares about the possible loss of her virginity, so that every pimply-faced, callow youth who dates her is viewed as a dangerous seducer. Mama, on the other hand, constantly cautions and coaches her on the horny ways of man, showing her every conceivable tactic for sexually attracting potential husbands of the professional level without "giving him what he really wants." The Princess is not discouraged from looking or acting sexy, she is merely given countless horrifying examples of what happens to Jewish girls who are reputed to be easy lays. Some of the examples are horrifying enough to cause traumatic chastity. I must add that the Mexican Princess is the exact replica of the Jewish Princess. In fact, almost every ethnic middle class produces this phenomenon. But the Jewish Princess is more notorious because there are more Jewish writers, most of whom have been victims of such charmers.

As for the Princess' brothers, they are much too involved playing the role of macho prince to care what happens to little sister.

## The Prince Syndrome

Just as papa creates a Princess, mama creates a Prince, with an occasional hand from fascinated sisters who may well be studying their brothers as test samples for their own subsequent dealings with such men. For the proud mother there is nothing too good for her son. She praises his good looks and lavishes him with constant affection and lots of good food, and she couldn't care less if he loses his virginity at an early age. Meanwhile, his father dutifully instructs him on how to make a good living, prods him to get a good education and furnishes whatever financial support he can. And quite often, with considerable wit, he will also instruct him on "how to get laid without getting the clap." With such parental care, it is small wonder that the son eventually becomes a rather demanding lover and/or husband. But, as a noted female psychoanalyst recently observed, most Jewish men seem to escape the Prince syndrome, so that there are many more princesses than princes. Her offhand estimate was a ratio of 4 to 1.

But an equally astute psychotherapist expressed a completely opposite view: "As far as I've been able to observe, that ratio is closer to one to one. There are probably just as many princes as princesses, except that the prince is much more passive. He quietly *expects* rather than demands; whereas the princess very outwardly demands. Any single woman on the West Side can tell you about some prince who goes from one woman's apartment to another, smilingly expecting to be fed and fucked, with no need to demand. It's his princely due."

All of which reminds me of the old Mexican joke about the mother who goes to Boston to visit her daughter Rosa and then to New York to visit her son Eduardo. On her return to Mexico City her best friend asks how her children are getting along with their new spouses.

"Well, let me tell you," says mama, "Rosa is married to the perfect husband. He washes the dishes, vacuums the floor, changes the baby's diapers and really does everything around the house."

"And what about Eduardo's wife?" asks her friend.

"Now that's another story. My poor Eduardo is married to this terrible little wench who forces him to wash dishes, change diapers . . ."

When I told this story to some Jewish friends in Cambridge many years ago, one of them insisted that it must be a Jewish joke about the proverbial Jewish mother. "But it can't be," I said with equal conviction. "It's so quintessentially Mexican. It's a perfect example of the Mexican mama." Yet one would have to admit that it was just as quintessentially Jewish . . . or Italian or Greek or Japanese. In others words, you don't have to be Jewish to be a mother.

## RELIGIOUS INFLUENCE ON SEX BEHAVIOR

Anyone raised in a Catholic family (especially if that family resides in a Chicano or Puerto Rican *barrio*) must be acutely aware of the sexual restraints that are a governing force in the Hispanic ethos. With an extremely hierarchical religion headed by a celibate Pope and presumably celibate priests and nuns, one must inevitably expect a heavy emphasis on the virtues of virginity and chastity and a concomitant sense of sinfulness and profound guilt. Indeed, sin and hoped-for redemption seem to be the yin and yang of Catholic consciousness, occasionally manifested in curious ways. One is reminded, for example, of voluptuous stripteasers in Mexico City solemnly making the Sign of the Cross and flinging their ebony crucifixes from bosom to back as they wait in the wings offstage, apparently asking forgiveness as they prepare to titillate a mostly male audience with sensuous bumps and grinds.

Like most Catholics, these strippers go to confession on Saturday afternoons and perhaps take Communion on Sunday morning, feeling somewhat absolved for the moment—but the guilt remains like an irremovable phantom presence. Admittedly, the burlesque strippers, and/or prostitutes, are perhaps the extreme example of this sex-guilt syndrome, but there are millions of Catholic women who are made to feel almost as guilty when they have sexual relations before marriage—or when they practice birth control during marriage itself. And, needless to say, abortion is the ultimate sin, often described as "murder" by the more vocal priests and lay believers.

As Marina Warner* recently put it, growing up Catholic was a "harrowing" experience:

*You didn't have to ask: anything remotely related to sex was wrong. In the ordeal of adolescence we fumbled our way toward adulthood through a maze of mortal sin. Damnation lurked in every lover's lane; conservative nuns and priests specialized in a genre of horror stories about couples who sinned mortally while parking, thinking they could later confess and wipe the slate clean. But alas, they died in a car accident on the way home, to be punished through all eternity for that moment of passion. The story was a favorite before proms and was frequently adapted to the local scene: in my home town, the nuns at the parochial school placed the parkers near the state mental hospital and did them in with an axe-wielding escapee.*

But even adult Catholics are traumatized by the rigidly stern sin ethic of the Church. One of my former colleagues had a prolonged affair with a thirty-year-old nurse whose fear of mortal sin eventually immobilized her. "We had sex two or three times a week for almost two years," he later confided, "but I literally had to force her every time—as if she were protecting her virginity with the most incredible resistance I had ever known. But the moment she gave in she would turn into a raving, insatiable wench, pleading for more and more, until I was completely drained. Then, suddenly, she would begin to cry and moan and call herself 'a damned whore,' and would carry on about committing mortal sin with a married man. And every Saturday afternoon she would go to confession and tell some priest about each transgression. But she would go to a different priest each time, going to eleven different churches and alternating between two and three priests in each church, so that no particular priest would hear her tearful confession more than twice a year."

Evidently unable to overcome her early Catholic training, her profound sense of sin, she finally terminated their relationship and apparently become celibate. As John Steinbeck might phrase it, "She had always been a virgin *by intention*, if not in fact."

Perhaps realizing that the burden of erotic sin was too

*Alone of Her Sex: The Myth and Cult of the Virgin Mary, Marina Warner, Alfred H. Knopf, 1976.

onerous for Catholics who came of age during the permissive 1960s, certain clergymen have recently tried to liberalize the Church's dictum on sexual morality. In a book-length study, *Human Sexuality: New Directions in American Catholic Thought*, a five-member committee of the Catholic Theological Society has said that the morality of all sexual acts is to be judged not by fixed rules but by whether they contribute "creative growth" and "integration of human personality" and are "honest, faithful, self-liberating, other-enriching, socially responsible, lifeserving and joyous."

Unfortunately, the Church hierarchy refused to accept the committee's views. In mid-November 1977, the National Conference of Catholic Bishops scoldingly assailed the study and once again reaffirmed their stand that sexual intercourse is morally right only within marriage and always wrong outside it. Moreover, the bishops approved a new national teaching guide which re-emphasized their condemnation of contraception and sterilization, further stressing the ancient Catholic dogma that "For a Christian, therefore, premarital sex, extramarital sex, adultery, homosexual behavior or other acts are strictly forbidden."

When one considers the high probability of homosexual behavior within the clergy itself, its rigid stand is especially ironic. But in tracing the development of Church teaching on homosexuality, a Yale University theologian, Dr. John Boswell, says that the Church was generally tolerant of homosexuality—and did not even classify it as a sin—until about 1200, when attitudes shifted dramatically. Boswell attributes this radical change to social changes in a Europe going through a time of great fear and insecurity, to which it responded by persecuting any type of nonconformity. It was, if you will, a medieval McCarthy era.

In England, for example, in about 1100, there was an unsuccessful effort to pass an ecclesiastical law to make homosexuality a sin. St. Anselm helped quash the proposed edict by arguing that, since no one had known such acts were sins, it was unfair to impose penalties after the fact. By 1290, less than 200 years later, homosexuality was not only a sin in England, but a crime punishable by death. (Similar penalties were imposed for sleeping with a Jew, Boswell says, which re-

minds him that twentieth-century American homophobia represents a departure from the patterns in Europe, where attacks
on gays have always coincided with persecution of Jews.
Though it is not well known, while Jews in Nazi Germany were
forced to wear yellow stars, homosexuals were branded with
pink triangles, and it is estimated that one out of four gay
Germans were exterminated in the camps.)

At any rate, Boswell's scholarly tome will challenge the
belief that homosexuality has been considered a grave sin
throughout the history of the Church.

Nevertheless, when one considers the Church's long-held
dogmas on all elements of sexual behavior, one would expect
sex to be equated with sin by certain overly conscientious
Catholics, especially as it relates to women. With the added
weight of machismo and its phobic emphasis on mandatory
virginity for prospective brides, one can well imagine the
psychic turmoil of Chicanas, Puertoriquenas and other *Latinas*
when confronted by passionate machos who insist on having
intercourse here and now, knowing full well that they will not
marry anyone whom they suspect is not a virgin.

Even if she were to resist actual intercourse, the Latin
female might feel compelled to confess to her priest that she
was *tempted* to commit fornication, which is a lesser offense but a
sin nonetheless, for which she might be given a penance of five
or ten Hail Marys. This quantification of sin is one of the more
amusing aspects of Catholicism. As a child, I once confessed to
masturbation, and the irate priest ordered me to say five Our
Fathers and five Hail Marys. My cousin Pablo subsequently
confessed to having intercourse with a waitress, and he was
ordered to say twenty Our Fathers and twenty Hail Marys—all
of which led me to the logical conclusion that fornication was
exactly four times more sinful than masturbation.

The Jewish religion may not quantify the various degrees
of sexual transgression; but like the Catholic Church, it certainly impinges upon the sexual behavior of its devotees.

Every day throughout the world, millions of Jewish men
utter a prayer thanking God for not creating them as women.
There are, of course, millions of non-Jewish men who feel the
same way, but their gratitude is not formalized in prayer. Although this "superior male" syndrome—with all its neurotic

elements—exists in every culture and every religion, its most explicit acceptance occurs in the Jewish religion. Since the Talmud was first written, nearly two thousand years ago, Jewish females have been considered inferior and thus assigned a second-class status in the religious rites and social customs of their people. And one must bear in mind that the Talmud was the written codification of traditional Jewish law and customs which had already been in force for 1,500 years.

In the words of Professor Paula Hyman, who teaches Modern Jewish History at Columbia University, "Judaism did not invent sexism, but it has had 3,500 years in which to perpetuate and legitimize sexist stereotypes, for the weight of tradition was paramount."

Throughout most of that long history, the Jewish ideal was the scholar, and the scholar was always a man. Women, in the eyes of most Jewish sages, were ignorant and frivolous and thus not capable of serious learning. Indeed, an old Talmudic saying explicitly expresses this notion: "Women are temperamentally light-headed." And as for anyone who dared think that his daughter might study the sacred texts, there was this harsh advice from Rabbi Eliezer in the Talmud itself: "Whoever teaches his daughter the Torah, teaches her obscenity"—no doubt meaning that the act of teaching her, rather than the Torah, was obscene.

Thus, marriage rather than scholarship was the proper function for women. Moreover, they should be passive, obedient brides; and this is a mandate even to this date, at least in Orthodox marriages. Witness, for example, the one-sided wedding ritual, where the groom does all the talking while the bride says nothing at all as the rabbi firmly announces that she is "consecrated unto her husband"—that is, forbidden sexually to other men. (In a polygamous society, her husband was not forbidden sexually to other women, unless they belonged to other husbands.) Nevertheless, the Jewish marriage contract commands the husband to protect and support his wife—and even to concern himself with her sexual needs.

According to Professor Hyman, "The authoritative 16th-century code of Jewish law, the *Shulhan Arukh*, stipulated the number of times per week, depending on his occupation, that a husband had to have intercourse with his wife. While a laborer was expected to perform twice a week, and a man of leisure every night, the pampered scholar had to meet his sexual obligations only once a week." One is tempted to speculate on the fornication quotas of morticians, lawyers and wigmakers.

But whatever his weekly quota might be, the husband was relieved of his sexual responsibilities when the wife had her menstrual period, a biological function that was regarded with fear and repugnance by rabbinical Judaism. Menstruation made a woman impure and she was therefore to be shunned by her husband. Even now, in Orthodox marriages, the husband and wife are told to separate from each other—no physical contact, separate beds—for the duration of the menstrual cycle plus seven days. And after this period has ended, the wife goes to a ritual bath called a *mikvah*, where she waits in line with the other women of her neighborhood. When her turn comes, she goes to one of several small rooms complete with bathtub, shower and sink. After showering or taking a bath, she goes into the mikvah, a small pool with lukewarm water about chest-deep, where she immerses herself three times and says two prayers. Following this ritual, she may go home and resume intercourse with her husband.

For Orthodox Jews a woman's sexuality has always been regarded as so threatening that it had to be shackled and/or removed from the male presence, with certain codes and customs designed to force female modesty. Deeply Orthodox Jews still think it immoral for a man to hear a woman sing, to look at her hair or to walk behind her on the street. With such fear of sexual attraction, it seems only logical to isolate women from such male functions as religious observance, which inevitably leads to an assumption of male superiority.

Consequently, as one would expect, the birth of a male child is cause for much celebration, while the birth of a baby girl generally causes no more than a stoic acceptance. In celebrating a boy's birth, the proud parents and relatives gather at the parents' home for a ritual called the *Bris*, wherein the infant is ceremoniously circumcised by a *mohel*, after which the celebrants happily drink to his future manhood.

## FEMALE REACTION TO CULTURAL AND RELIGIOUS EXCLUSION AND PUT-DOWNS———

In a *MS.* magazine article titled "The View from the Back of the Shul," Audrey Gellis records her reactions to the absence of a celebration when she was born:

*When I was a little girl, I asked my mother why God didn't like girls. I was too young to understand the ritual significance of my baby brother's bris (circumcision ceremony), but even as a five-year-old I knew all that fuss wasn't for simply snipping a piece of skin off an infant's penis. I was aware that there was a big party at the hospital, with all our relatives and friends drinking* schnaaps *and congratulating my glowing father on having a son. I knew that something powerful (if frightening) was happening to my baby brother.*

*"Did you have a party when I was born?" I asked my mother. Nothing. My grandfather had gone to* shul *(synagogue) alone and tipped the rabbi to say a prayer in my Hebrew name, Elka (Elka, meaning "gift of God"—some way to treat a gift of God). "Why wasn't there a party?" "You weren't a boy, dear." I was the firstborn child but there was nothing to celebrate when I was born. Had I been a boy, there would have been not only a* bris *but a* pidyon haben, *a reenactment of the purchase of the son in lieu of his entering the service of God.*

*I threw a tantrum that night because there was no* pidyon haben *when I was born, and 20 years later a male Jewish shrink told me I had penis envy.*

Several theories have been adduced to explain the ancient rite of circumcision. Maimonides, the famous rabbinical scholar of the twelfth century, believed that God had mandated the circumcision of the Jews so as to reduce raging passions. "One of its objects," he wrote, "is to limit intercourse and to weaken the organ of generation as far as possible, and thus cause men to be moderate. The organ necessarily becomes weak when it loses blood and is deprived of its covering from the beginning."

On the other hand, Herodotus much earlier (500 B.C.) had said that the Egyptians believed in circumcision because they preferred cleanliness to beauty. Thus, despite Maimonides, it was this emphasis on hygiene that was stressed by Jewish writers, who felt that the Bible somehow foresaw the lower incidence of carcinoma in the *glans penis* of the circumcised males, less carcinoma of the female cervix and an absence of phymosis. But in the words of Ernest Van den Haag, "Anachronistic thinking of this sort—sometimes used as well to explain Jewish dietary laws—assumes that desert tribes followed scientific methods, and ignores the anthropological evidence which suggests magical and totemic beliefs underlying both the widespread dietary laws and the custom of circumcision."

In his classic treatise on phallic worship, G. R. Scott states that "the mutilation of the genital appealed to the peoples as an eminently satisfactory means of offering a part of the body which would be most appreciated by the deity." Van den Haag goes one step further when he says, "At least one god who is to be mollified by this symbolic castration is not as far away as heaven. The child's father is right there, at the ceremony." This view is at least partially shared by certain psychoanalysts who theorize that the birth of a son arouses not only love and pride, but a certain degree of anger and anxiety in the father, who now finds himself sharing his wife's love and attention with a formidable rival.

The operation itself is simple and brief. The foreskin is quickly cut from the *glans* while the mohel solemnly says: "O Living God, command to preserve our beloved flesh from destruction"—which clearly means that the severed piece of flesh has been sacrificed to preserve the rest of the penis. If perchance the infant is born without a foreskin, the mohel will nevertheless scratch him with a knife so as to draw a trickle of blood.

Although one might well expect a certain psychological sequel from such a solemn and exacting ritual, only a very few of my male Jewish respondents (less than 5 percent) expressed any conscious reaction to their having been circumcised. Most of them simply assumed that it was merely an act of hygienic precaution. None were willing to accept Maimonides' grim notion that circumcision was meant to "limit intercourse and to weaken the organ of generation."

## BAR MITZVAH AS A MACHO CEREMONY_____

About 60 percent of the Jewish female interviewees expressed a considerable resentment of the male-centered rites of circumcision, but an even more resentful 85 percent recalled the favoritism shown their brothers in the far more publicized rite called the *Bar Mitzvah*, in which the thirteen-year-old boy suddenly becomes a man. Later, as mothers, they felt a different but just as painful sense of exclusion, as will be noted in these comments:

> "My brother was such a snot at his *Bar Mitzvah*. You'd think that he had just been crowned or made a Pope. And then he got all these presents—nine fountains pens yet, three watches, four fancy tie pins, and all kinds of loot. Just because he was thirteen years old and was supposed to be a man!"
>
> *Mother:* "I felt like a nothing at the temple, sitting there like a mere spectator while my damned husband took center stage with my son Irving. It was strictly a male thing. Even his grandfather and two uncles got into the act, while I just sat there with nothing to do. Of course I knew how it would be, with all that tradition, but I still couldn't help feeling sort of left out."
>
> *Mother:* "I got the job of ordering all the food and getting the dance band, and all the usual female obligations. But at the actual *Bar Mitzvah* in the temple, you wouldn't know I existed. It was only the men who counted. You wouldn't know Aaron had a mother."
>
> *Mother:* "I only got mentioned once in the whole ceremony, and that was just in passing, when the rabbi said something about the son of Sam and Debby Rosen. That was the only recognition I got at the temple."
>
> "It's strictly a macho trip—like everything else that happens in the Jewish religion. Take, for example, that crap about, 'Thank you, God, for making me a man.' Every time I hear my husband say that damned prayer, I want to vomit."
>
> "I'll tell you why I won't go to the temple, even during the High Holy Days. Why should I sit in the balcony like the colored people in the movies when I was a kid?"

## BAS MITZVAH AS A TOKEN RITE FOR GIRLS ____

Perhaps yielding to feminist pressures, some temples now have *Bas Mitzvahs* for girls; but compared with Bar Mitzvahs, these female rituals seem to be mere tokenism, since they may involve several (if not many) thirteen-year-old girls and thus lack the concentrated exclusivity of the Bar Mitzvah.

Considering all these various complications that have their genesis in a male-oriented religion, one can easily understand why many Jews differ from non-Jews with respect to sexual attitudes and behavior. Reform Jews differ considerably from their Orthodox and Conservative brethren, but even they have not completely escaped the push and pull of a long heritage of female exclusion.

The sexual attitudes and behavior of Protestants, particularly those from New England and the South, have also been heavily influenced by the moral restrictions of the various Protestant churches. The so-called WASPs of New England, though no longer adhering to the religious principles of the awesome Cotton Mather, nonetheless retain a certain Puritan ethos with respect to sex. Aside from a psychic restraint (or uptightness) in their relations with the opposite sex, they seem to have a general aversion to bodily contact. Even when they shake hands with good friends, they do so quickly and/or tentatively, as if fearing an exchange of germs or an erotic impulse. This is particularly true of WASP males, whom one would never expect to embrace in public as do the Italian and Irish Catholics who now outnumber them in such places as Boston and Providence.

This personal austerity and almost phobic sense of privacy may be traced to Calvinist strictures against the sins of the flesh, which could best be avoided by the deliberate omission of human contact. (What better way to assure such isolation than the legendary "bundling board," the wooden plank down the center of the bed which separated an engaged couple on cold nights when they had to crawl under blankets to avoid freezing to death.) This actual or symbolic isolation, this taciturn avoidance of spontaneous social intercourse, has been graphically expressed—almost with religious solemnity—in Robert Frost's memorable injunction that "good fences make good neighbors." Indeed, many New Englanders seem to carry their fences (or bundling boards) with them, perhaps as a precaution against themselves, against some errant erotic impulse that might prove uncontrollable if permitted even the slightest momentary escape.

Several years ago, for example, the WASP wife of a WASP Boston lawyer told a psychiatric interviewer that she had been wanting to have an extramarital affair for at least a decade, that she had dreamed of going to bed with at least fifteen men in their social circle, but that she had "always frozen stiff" when any man touched her. "I seem to have this invisible chastity belt that I can't take off," she said with no little anguish in her voice, continuing:

*And it's been there ever since I can remember. In fact, everyone in my family and all my relatives had this thing of not touching each other. Even when I went to dance classes on Saturdays, we would all dance as far apart from partners as possible, with our bodies never touching, and the boy's right hand barely grazing your back so that there was no sense of his leading you. It was the most sexless dancing you can possibly imagine, but I'd go home aching with desire.*

*It was the same way at Radcliffe—I'd have to get drunk before any man could touch me; and I envied my roommate, this Italian girl from Rhode Island, who could neck for hours without going all the way. But she had no fear of her body, and she loved physical contact—with man or woman. Yet whenever she hugged me, or even touched my arm in a casual way, I would sort of freeze. It was easier being with some of my old friends from Chestnut Hill and Back Bay, because they weren't the huggy type like Catholics tend to be. Well, I finally had sex with the man I finally married, and we both were pretty drunk when it happened. As a matter of fact, he's so damned uptight about sex that he has to have a few drinks before anything happens. And, of course, he never does any foreplay, never touches me where the sex books say I'm supposed to be touched.*

There are, of course, varying degrees of this don't-touch syndrome, and many New England WASPs are entirely free of the restrictive Puritan ethos. Among the more emancipated are the upper-income inhabitants of avant-garde communities such as Ipswich, Massachusetts, the ill-disguised locale of John Updike's *Couples*, most of whom spent hours of erotic dalliance on various beds and couches with whatever lover might be available at a given moment. But as one Ipswicher confided to an old friend, "Most of us need a lot of booze or pot to really loosen up—I mean sexually."

Lacking both of these stimulants, the Christian Scientists in that region are perhaps the most strait-laced Protestants, often resembling the Mormons in their aversion to sensual pleasures. They are also the least likely to discuss their sex lives, so that there is a paucity of verifiable data on specific behavior.

Southern Baptists, on the other hand, are much less reluctant to talk about sex, but much of their talk consists of vehement proclamations of resisted temptation. Rural preachers are especially adept at describing the lurid pitfalls of sex, their accounts often hinting of personal exposure and subsequent redemption à la Elmer Gantry. Indeed, the redeemed sinner is held in high regard. Almost as highly esteemed are those who publicly confess to great and continuing temptations, all of which conjure up visions of moral turmoil and ultimate victory over the forces of Satan. Thus, to the average Southern Baptist, Jimmy Carter's admission of an occasional "lust in my heart" for other women was no surprise, while many people outside the South expressed shocked disapproval. "Hell's bell's," said one Georgian, "Jimmy was just being honest, and a whole slew of hypocrites are jumping on him as if they ain't never been tempted by a neighbor's wife."

The soulful and confessional lyrics of the Country & Western music that blares from millions of radios throughout the South (and, increasingly, all other regions) express a sexual ethos that seems to be an admixture of Baptist hell-fire and old Southern gallantry, which decrees that men must defend the "honor" of their women at all costs. And in their fear of the mythic virility of black men, white Southern males have often tried to emasculate these potential despoilers of Southern womanhood, quite often quoting the Bible to justify the most venal acts.

Perhaps plagued by real or imagined sexual impotence, many Southerners resort to violence to assert their manliness, frequently carrying guns at their hips or inside their cars. The late Elvis Presley, for example, had a collection of 150 firearms of all makes and models—which brings to mind the theory that guns are phallic symbols, surrogate penises. This, in turn, evokes the memory of Warren Beatty as the hairdresser in *Shampoo*, wearing his pistol-like hair dryer on his hip like a cowboy and using the dryer to suggest an act of fellatio by Julie Christie, presumably establishing his credentials as a real macho.

The most extreme manifestations of Southern machismo can be found in the state of Texas, where Lyndon Baines Johnson was a prime example of manly pride. For LBJ, the ultimate symbol of cherished womanhood was his mother, whom he revered (and feared) with an almost mawkish intensity. And like many mother-worshippers, he had a driving need to prove he was "all man," perhaps more manly than his daddy, which often resulted in embarrassing displays of sexual potency that soon became legends on Capitol Hill.

As one might expect, such excessive male pride occasionally masks an incipient homosexuality which most Southerners consider an irredeemable curse. In 1978, for example, the incumbent Democratic governor of Oklahoma was accused of homosexuality by one of his primary opponents and was challenged by another opponent to publicly declare whether he was either homosexual or bisexual. Though defeating both men rather handily, Governor Boren felt compelled to deny the accusations in a subsequent televised program. Conscious of his mostly Baptist constituency, he placed a white Bible on a podium in full view of the cameras and made the following statement:

*I, David Boren, being of lawful age and upon my oath, do swear and state that I know what homosexuals and bisexuals are. I further swear that I am not a homosexual or bisexual. And I further swear that I have never engaged in any homosexual or bisexual activities, nor do I approve or condone them.*

*With my hand on the Bible which was used in my inaugural ceremony, I want to publicly affirm the statement that I have already made under oath.*

The Bible is a familiar prop for Southern politicians, and religious affirmations occur in the most unlikely places by the most unlikely people. Kelly Everts, a buxom stripteaser known to thousands of male fans throughout the so-called Bible Belt, frequently spends her free afternoons preaching sermons against sin and liquor. Seeing no contradiction between her profession and her professions, she sincerely says that "I have come to realize that stripteasing is my calling in life. Now I understand that it's my duty to be beautiful to men, to be a symbol of feminine beauty to them."

Having recently preached the gospel to 300 people on the grounds of the White House in Washington, D.C., Ms. Evert told reporters that she was happy with President Carter "because he's a man of God." She also said, "When Nixon was in office, God tried to reach him, but he wouldn't listen. I believe the Watergate scandal was an act of God to put Nixon out of office and to eventually get a godly person there. President Carter is that person."

## MOTHER PRESSURES_____

Aside from the heavy influence of religion in the formation of early sexual attitudes, societal and family pressures are a dominant force—and the mother is usually the conduit of such pressures. It is she who guides the child, either girl or boy, in her/his initial orientation to gender roles.

It is interesting to note in this respect that most "liberated mothers" continue to raise their sons as conventional little machos while trying to train their daughters to resist machismo. Here, for example, is an excerpt from a study conducted by Lindsay Van Gelder and Carrie Carmichael, as reported in *MS.* magazine:

*The underlying assumption was that the typical male personality is the ideal— and that it's exclusively up to us, the mothers of girls, to equalize things by making out daughters more "active" or "masculine." We heard a lot about the joys of buying football helmets for little girls. But when we asked these women what they were doing to make their sons less like typical males, we either drew a blank or an antihomosexual response.*

*We found that plenty of women who rail against male privilege in their own lives are happy to capitalize on it where their boy children are concerned. If their sons have an edge in life because they're males . . . well, yes, it may not be fair, but that's life, and we all want our kids to succeed, right? As the mothers of daughters, we began to feel that when our children reach womanhood in the early 1990s they will be confronted with a new generation of perfectly preserved 1960s males.*

To illustrate their point, they quote a young mother who is an avowed and militant feminist, who nonetheless backs off from her principles when it comes to rearing her three adolescent boys:

*If I had the powers to make a child into a liberated non-male chauvinist, I don't know whether I would do it. You cannot alienate the child from his culture. My sons are developing many features that are most distasteful to me. They have contempt for women. They have very much objectified women as sex objects. They sit around reading* Playboy. *I try to counteract without breaking their backs or making them react in the opposite direction. Every time there is a chance for me to point out to them the deficiencies of their society, I do it, but the child has to make his final choice. I love them. I cannot get myself to look at them as my enemy.*

But the most poignant remark is that of the supposedly liberated mother who, upon seeing her newborn child, reacted as if she had never been exposed to Women's Lib: "When he was born and the doctor held him up in the palms of his hands, all I could see was his *prick*. It looked enormous to me. When he was a tiny baby, on the changing table, I remember feeling he was a little *king*. Because of his penis, his maleness, he had a power over me, he intimidated me."

Quite obviously, the male-female dichotomy has been firmly planted in this woman's psyche—and, perhaps, to a lesser degree, in the psyche of millions of other women. Some have inwardly rebelled; others have accepted their submissive roles with apparent good will. Take, for example, the wife of a Milwaukee rabbi who comes from a family (the Twerskis) that boasts ten successive generations of rabbis. Asserting in a newspaper interview that a woman's natural function is motherhood and keeping a nice home, she says: "It bothers me when I see friends trying to get into a man's world. And to me it's insignificant compared to what we have in life. For a woman to become an executive—what lives on after it? What mark does she leave on eternity? With children and home you leave a mark on a human being, not on papers or an office. . . ."

One can better understand Feige Twerski's attitude when one realizes that she was raised in an Orthodox ambiance that assigns specific roles to each sex from the very outset. Indeed, children have almost no independence in matters relating to boy-girl relations. There is seldom any dating, and all marriages are arranged. Thus, at the age of eleven, the elder Twerski (Jacob) was engaged to Leah, then nine—and they did not meet until their wedding day. When the marriage took place, he moved to her home in Poland from his native village of Gornostaipol, in Russia. Soon thereafter they moved to Milwaukee and brought all their traditions with them.

But there were some changes, according to Jacob's son Michael (also a rabbi). "You can have a totally arranged marriage, where nobody sees nobody—or you can have a limited, not overindulgent exposure. I saw Feige before our marriage on more than one occasion."

"Three, to be exact," said Feige.

"Our parents were sitting close by," added her husband.

"If Feige had decided she didn't want to marry me it would have posed a problem for me, but not for her. Her father would not have forced her to marry me."

Needless to say, there is no sex prior to such arranged marriages—no way of knowing if the couples are sexually compatible. But because of her restrictive childhood conditioning, Feige Twerski inevitably accepted the parental arrangement and has willingly become a dutiful mother and homemaker, with no wish to "intrude" on the terrain assigned to menfolk. And if her daughters remain within the circumscribed Orthodox community, they too will accept the same prescribed female roles.

In these days of "liberated sex" among the young, even the daughters of Orthodox rabbis and Protestant clergymen might find it difficult to resist the lure of premarital intercourse. Although there are no firm statistics on sexual behavior in junior and senior high schools in such avant-garde communities as Beverly Hills, Marin County, Westchester, Ipswich and Grosse Point, one can assume that these students begin their sexual education fairly early. Indeed, in certain enclaves within our society, American young may be ahead of the youngsters in the legendary swinging society of Sweden. According to a recent survey by the Karolinska Hospital in Stockholm, the average Swedish male loses his virginity at the age of 17.4 years, and females at 15.8 years. Approximately 20 percent of the eighteen-year-old girls in the random sample said they used no contraceptives, and 6 percent admitted a first sexual experience at the age of twelve. More than one-third of both sexes described their initial intercourse as a disappointing experience. "I was glad to get it over and done with," one girl told an interviewer. "The experience certainly didn't equal the expectation."

# 2
# The Sexual Behavior of Adult Females

*The differences in being, having and doing are crucial in existentialism. In "The Dread of Women," Karen Horney discussed their implications for men and women in the sexual act. The woman "performs her part by merely being, without any doing—a fact that has always filled men with admiration and resentment. The man, on the other hand, has to do something to fulfill himself." It is not enough for him to have a penis in the sexual encounter, his being and that of his partner must be affirmed in his doing.*

HELPING PEOPLE: Karen Horney's Psychoanalytic Approach
—Harold Kelman, M.D.

Contrary to what is generally believed, most Jewish women are not afflicted by the Jewish Princess syndrome—certainly no more than women in other cultures are afflicted by their own version of the princess phenomenon. But for those who are affected (and I should note that only 34 percent of my Jewish interviewees and 30 percent of my gentile interviewees would admit to being princesses), the symptoms hang on for a long time. For example, more than 50 percent of the male interviewees (both gentile and Jewish) complained that their wives were grown-up princesses, whose demands had steadily escalated year by year:

"My wife, she never lets up. It's gimme this, gimme that. And nothing ever satisfies her. The only thanks I ever get in my life is from this nice shiksa model at my factory. Now she knows how to appreciate!"

33

"Listen, I never yet met an Italian wife who wasn't already a princess. Take my Maria, for example. She wants everything, and nothing can please her. So what are you going to do when you got not only a princess but the crown princess herself."

"I could tell from the minute the honeymoon started that I had married into the nobility of Forest Hills. To begin with, she didn't like the hotel I picked, then the food wasn't good enough for her and the dance band was too loud and vulgar. And finally, she didn't like the way I screwed. She just looked at me when it was over and said, 'Is that all there is? What everybody is always raving about?' Well, I guess it could have been worse. At least I knew she was a virgin."

Not surprisingly, many of our Catholic and Protestant male respondents felt that their gentile girl friends and wives were just as demanding, if not quite so colorfully vocal, as the Jewish women they had been involved with. More than 60 percent of this group went on to say that they preferred Jewish women even when they were princesses.

"Look, any woman makes demands, no matter what her religion or nationality. But now Jewish women are up front about it. They don't just sit around and mope and give you that blank stare of disapproval like my wife does. Hell, they let you know what's on their minds, and you can deal with it—or try to."

"I've known two or three of these so-called Jewish princesses; and I'd take them over some of the Catholics and Protestants I've been with. These Jewish broads make demands all right—just like any woman will—but, hell, they're at least funny about it. You don't have to guess what they don't like or what's bothering them—they'll just tell you."

With considerable justification, many adult females resent the negative portrayals which have attached to them simply because they are Jewish and women. One such person is Audrey Gellis, author of the *MS.* magazine article "The View from the Back of the Shul," previously cited:

*When I was 10, gangs of hoods would throw stones at us Jewish kids on the way home from cheder. Occasionally a stone hit me. Yet none of those young bullies ever hurt me as much as the grown Jewish men who have called me a JAP— Jewish American Princess.*

*I knew what was wrong, but I didn't dare say the obvious—the real JAP was the Jewish American Prince. I had evidence in my own family and corrob-oration from the boys and men I'd known for many years. The fact is: the man comes first.*

*My mother and my aunt dropped out of high school so my uncle could go to medical school; a generation later my parents talked me out of law school and begged my brother to go to medical school . . . I did go to college (and it must be said in fairness that among working- and middle-class families, Jews were the first to send their daughters to college* en masse). *But my goals were clearly limited: become a schoolteacher and look for a husband. However, much as I may have been stalking a man, the budding princes weren't exactly lining up for a frizzy-haired Jewish girl from the Bronx. I learned that Jewish medical and law fraternities "mixed" only with the best (meaning "rich girl") Jewish sororities.*

*Like all upwardly mobile men, Jewish men choose wives who are status symbols, and in our society that means tall, slender blondes.*

*The Jewish male doesn't suffer from any of the image problems that plague us. He's billed as sexy, brilliant, a good provider, and the world's best husband. Pursued by both Jew and gentile, he doesn't fail to let you know how lucky you are to date him.*

Ms. Gellis' sentiments are but an echo of the almost identical resentment expressed by some of my Catholic and Protestant female interviewees. Their comments ran the gamut from amused irony to smoldering range:

"I am not a spoiled cock-teasing bitch, and I never have been. It's just that most men can't stand to be rejected—especially a macho—so then he has to salve his ego by calling you names."

"Sure, my dad used to call me his princess; but when the real crunch came, it was my younger brother who got all the favors, who got sent to law school, who got more money for school. Nobody called him a prince, but he was sure treated that way."

"My mother was always warning me not to put out, to save myself. She kept telling me that no Chicano man will marry an easy lay; and on the morning of my wedding she said, 'Don't let him know you like the sex part—otherwise he'll think you have had experience.' So I had to fake all this innocence."

Since teasing-without-yielding is a major facet of the Princess image, perhaps we should bear that factor in mind as we analyze the sexual behavior of adult Jewish females as compared with Catholic and Protestant females. In so doing, we have covered a wide range of activity and/or attitudes, including penis envy; masturbation; petting to climax; fantasies and nocturnal emissions; intercourse with males; pregnancy and abortion; clitoral versus vaginal orgasm; oral sex with male or female; response to cunnilingus by male or female; the use of dildos, vibrators and other objects; the use of erotic, bawdy language; lesbian relationships; sado-masochism; reaction to pornographic films and literature; and sexual contact with animals.

## PENIS ENVY

About 60 percent of the women interviewed, Jewish and gentile alike, accept Sigmund Freud's now classic formulation that the female clitoris is an inferior penis, which naturally produces penis envy.

Before proceeding further, I should like to offer a dissent from Dr. Freud's macho theory. First of all, to compare the clitoris with the penis is like comparing grapes and apples and concluding that grapes are inferior because they are smaller. The clitoris and penis are indeed erogenous organs, but so are ears, nipples, elbows, thighs, palms and many other parts of the human body. And if some Freudian enthusiast should triumphantly announce that Freud's penis-clitoris analogy is valid because both are subject to erection when fondled, he also would have to include breast nipples. But has anyone ever argued that a nipple is an inferior penis? As Gertrude Stein might have said, "A penis is a penis is a penis—and a clitoris is a clitoris is a clitoris." What more anatomical proof is needed than the mere fact that a clitoris has no urinary function and does not excrete semen? May I further suggest that women are also endangering their psychic health when they refer to auto-clitoral-stimulation as "masturbation,"* because in so doing they are once again accepting a word that is directly related to a penis, and this inevitably leads to invidious comparisons. Wouldn't it suffice or say "fondle" or "stimulate" rather than "masturbate"?

But getting back to the previously mentioned 60 percent of women who did accept the notion that their clitoral organs

---

*I have used the term "masturbation" in this context to follow literary convention, but I still believe it is inaccurate.

were inferior to the male penis, I found a varied melange of emotions and attitudes dredged from the past with varying degrees of reluctance and occasional embarrassment. The following recollections were picked at random with no attempt to stress any particular point of view:

"I was terribly jealous of my brother's penis, especially when it got bigger and bigger as he masturbated. He used to call it jacking-off, which I considered a very funny word—and still do. But to tell you the real truth. I don't particularly feel jealous about my husband's penis—probably because he seldom gets an erection. At least not around me."

"My sister and I used to see our cousins jerking off and sometimes coming all over their pants. Even though it got sort of messy, I still wished I could have a penis, so I could jerk off. Now that I'm masturbating fairly regularly, I don't feel at all jealous about not having a penis."

"Well, even when your clit gets hard and you get that fantastic crazy feeling, as if it's going to take off like a space rocket, you sometimes get the feeling that his orgasm was greater because his big cock had more juice. I feel that way when my husband comes and he lets out a crazy wild moan, as if he's getting more pleasure than I am, just because his thing is bigger than mine."

## MASTURBATION

Until recent years, most men in this country did not know that their wives, lovers, sisters and daughters regularly engage in masturbation. Perhaps even now, many will refuse to believe so despite several authoritative reports which indicate that about nine out of ten females masturbate on a periodic basis. This vast male ignorance is undoubtedly due to long-established taboos against women openly discussing sex, even among themselves. My data show that 90 percent of the adult Jewish females interviewed have at some time or other stimulated their genital organs, as compared with 85 percent of the Catholic interviewees—and that slight differential could easily be attributed to the fact that the Jewish respondents were generally more willing to talk about their sexual behavior. Take, for example, the following comments from several females ranging from twenty to fifty-six years of age:

"I've been married thirty-six years, but my husband still doesn't know that I play with myself. It would have been fun to do it during intercourse, and once or twice I was about to suggest it, but I guess I was afraid he'd think something bad about me. So I've just kept it to myself. And I wouldn't be telling you if I hadn't read about it in Masters and Johnson."

"It seems so natural to do it. Why have I felt so guilty?"

"Look, I've been doing it since I was a child—secretly, of course—but then I saw my eight-year-old daughter fingering herself, and I yelled like a witch at her. It really upset me even though I've been told it's perfectly natural."

"Well, I finally told my husband that I've been masturbating since before we got married, and that really bugged him. He wouldn't touch me for a whole week, and I couldn't get him to read these articles about women's sexuality."

"Now that I've been reading so much about other women masturbating, I don't feel guilty anymore. I even talked about it with this woman I met at the local laundromat. But she made the mistake of telling her husband, and he gave her a black eye. Called her a goddamned pervert."

"My husband now knows that I play with myself, and he keeps kidding me about my little prick, which I don't think is at all funny."

"I've been playing with my clit a long time, but I still feel sort of guilty about it. And I get mad at myself for feeling guilty because there's really nothing wrong with it. It's as natural as eating or blowing your nose, or any other physical act."

Now that women have become more aware of the nearly universal practice of female masturbation—either through conversations with friends or through reading Masters and Johnson, the recent Hite Report, and other pertinent literature—they may begin to resolve some of the emotional conflicts that arise therefrom. But they will still be faced with the delicate problem of the masculine ego, which impedes their husband's and lover's understanding of female sexuality.

## PETTING TO CLIMAX

Although petting to climax (which was known as "necking to come" in my generation) has usually been considered a teenage activity, there are quite a few adult females who indulge in such behavior well into their forties. About 15 percent of Protestant interviewees and 20 percent of Jewish interviewees admitted engaging in this type of activity at least once after marriage or after reaching the age of twenty-five if unmarried. This 4-to-3 ratio may be traced to a residue of the tease-but-don't-screw tactic which many Jewish females learn in puberty, or it may simply reflect a greater willingness to talk about sex in any of its various aspects, as can be seen in the following comments:

"I still get a charge out of getting some guy all hot and bothered with a little tongue juice."

"This professor—a real famous one—grabbed me in the pantry and started smooching like a teenager. So I gave him the best dry fuck he ever had—except it wasn't so dry, because he got his come all over his pant leg."

"Look, I'm not a teenager—as a matter of fact, I'm over thirty—but I still do a lot of hot necking with men I don't want to lay. It's just a convenient way to satisfy both our needs without going all the way."

"During a drunken weekend out in the Hamptons, one of my husband's business connections (some WASP from Boston) started necking with me in the kitchen while everyone else was down at the beach. So when I told him I couldn't go all the way because he didn't have a condom, he started wrapping his stiff pecker with Saran Wrap, but he came all over his hands before he could wrap it on. Which solved my problem, what can I tell you."

"I've always said that a hot juicy tongue is just as good as a wet pussy, and not nearly as complicated. All a man wants is to come, no matter how you do it."

"I really do like to neck. I like it better than intercourse. And I especially like to neck with some Guy Lombardo music in the background—like at a high-school prom at Frank Daley's old Meadowbrook Club in Jersey."

"This Italian came up to me in this bar, and when we shook hands he started tickling my palm and getting me all hot and bothered. He didn't have to kiss me or anything else—that tickling my palm was all he needed."

Apparently most people discontinue petting to climax after reaching maturity and/or getting married. They may occasionally neck furiously with someone other than their spouses at a party, but seldom *with* their spouses at home. There is, of course, some degree of quick petting as a prelude to intercourse, since petting is usually considered as a mere preliminary step in an overall process. In a most persuasive article titled "Treating Goal-Directed Intimacy,"* Richard L. Timmers, Lloyd G. Sinclair and June Rea James warn against this stepladder approach to sex, in which the hierarchy is often a series of acts that progresses through touching, kissing, caressing, insertion and, finally, orgasm:

*There are several dangers in following the stepladder approach to shared intimacy. Frequently the sequence of events is followed so rigidly that in focusing solely on intercourse and orgasm, the couple minimizes or negates the importance of foreplay. If anything goes wrong in following the hierarchical scale, or if the goals of intercourse and orgasm are not met, the entire experience is considered a failure. Partners often do not permit themselves to touch, caress, hug, or hold each other unless they are prepared to proceed to intercourse and orgasm. When the same behaviors are repeated each time, boredom ensues, sexual interest declines, and the attention and energy of the partners becomes consumed by a vigilant observation of one another's performance to insure that each is following the correct steps.*

The authors have conceived of a circular view of sexual interaction that discourages a hierarchical framework of behaviors. (See Figure.) The major points of this restructuring of attitudes is outlined as follows:

> Touching, holding, kissing and caressing, in addition to penis-vagina contact, can be viewed as sex play and not as foreplay. This significant attitudinal change is necessary to begin to help the person discard goal-directed behaviors.
>
> Through a focus on the feelings and needs of the moment, clients learn to value all aspects of sex play. One example of this is the sensate focus experiences described by Masters and Johnson.
>
> Acceptance of the need to share individual feelings—without the pressured expectations that "something has to happen next"—legitimizes those needs and permits couples to communicate feelings more effectively.
>
> Couples create their own unique "circle" of intimacy in which all aspects of the shared experience have value.
>
> If all components of the circle have value, the shared experience does not necessarily lead to one particular goal, and the experience cannot be a failure.

*Printed in *Social Work*, Journal of the National Association of Social Workers, Vol. 21, No. 5, September 1976.

*Comparison of Two Attitudes*
*Toward Shared Sexuality*

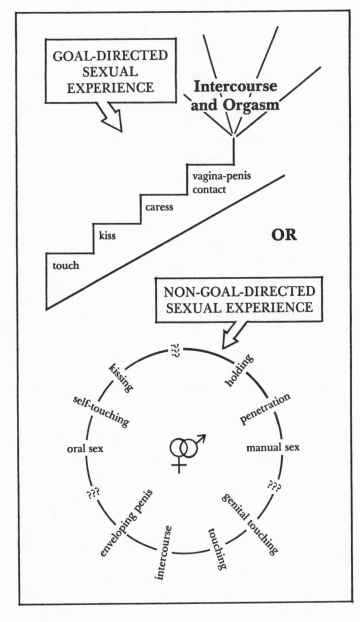

Different sensations certainly feel different. However, no functional purpose is served in ranking them as a preliminary to another.

## RESPONSE TO CLITORAL
## STIMULATION BY PARTNER

Since most men consider vaginal arousal more important than clitoral arousal (indeed, some of them seem not to know where the clitoris is), many women fail to get the kind of erotic satisfaction they want and need. Even those men who actually engage in manual clitoral stimulation generally regard this activity as foreplay, as a mere prelude to intercourse, seldom realizing that the female partner fairly aches for a clitoral orgasm before intercourse. Consequently, some sexologists have expressed surprise on reading the recent Hite Report, which flatly states that 44 percent of American women regularly achieve orgasm through manual stimulation by a partner.

Since Ms. Hite makes no distinction between male and female partners, some of the questionnaire answers clearly indicating lesbian relationships, one cannot estimate how many of her respondents experienced manual clitoral orgasm with a male partner. My data suggest that 20 percent of the Jewish interviewees and 15 percent of the gentile interviewees regularly achieve orgasm in this manner, which would lead us to assume that Jewish men engage in more creative (or at least less inhibited) foreplay than their gentile counterparts. Almost 100 percent of these women have also attained climax through masturbation, often more quickly and more easily. The 80 percent or 85 percent who have not had this experience with male lovers (and/or husbands) have in numerous ways expressed their longing, resentment or resigned indifference:

"I've always wanted my husband to play with my clit, but I've been afraid to ask him because it might make him think some other man has done that to me."

"When my husband started playing with my clit—I mean after years of concentrating on my vagina—I wondered if some other woman had taught him; but I decided not to ask him. That's because it felt so good; I didn't give a damn where he had learned to do it. But I still wonder who taught him."

"My girl friend kept bragging about how her husband could make her come by just playing with her clit, so I finally asked her to tell her husband to tell *my* husband how to do it, which she did. But when a few weeks went by and my husband hadn't changed, I finally asked him if men ever talk to each other about how they make love to their wives. 'Why should we?' he asked with this funny look in his eyes. 'What you do with your wife is private, it's your own damn business. Jesus, Alice, you don't talk about that kinda stuff.' That may be true, but I happen to know that they tell an awful lot of dirty stories and also do a lot of bragging about sex with other women."

"This French doctor once told me that 'American men know everything about a carburetor and nothing about a clitoris,' which sounds pretty true to me. It's certainly true about my husband."

"My lover starts playing with my clit and I start going crazy— really crazy, like I'm about to come—then he suddenly leaves my clit and climbs on me for a quick screw. And afterwards, he just lies there, obviously convinced that I'm as satisfied as he is, and I just go along with all that crappy pretense."

"Once, just once, I wish my guy would stay on my clit till I really come. But he always thinks that a wet vagina is a sure sign that I'm ready."

"This female doctor made me come with just her little finger, and we were lovers for a while. Of course, I'd rather have a man do it, but sometimes . . ."

"Listen, my husband is the Jascha Heifetz of the clitoris. With his fantastic light fingers, why should I need his clumsy penis? As for intercourse, I do it strictly for him. He's entitled."

As one can readily see, there is a wide range of response to clitoral stimulation by a male or female partner, with a possibility of variable satisfaction produced by outside advice by friends or sexual therapists. But the limits of escalation or de-escalation are set forth in the graph (see page 44) devised by Natalie Shainess, M.D., whose article, "Authentic Feminine Response," should be required reading for anyone concerned with this complex phenomenon.

While on this subject, Dr. Shainess cites Freud's now-much-disputed statement on clitoral orgasm in his essay "The Transformation of Puberty" and states the following about the clitoris:

*Its role is to conduct the excitement to the adjacent genital parts; it acts like a chip of pinewood which is utilized to set fire to the harder wood. It often takes some time before this transference is accomplished. . . . This anesthesia [vaginal] may become permanent if the clitoris refuses to give up its excitability. . . . If the transference of the erogenous excitability from the clitoris to the vagina succeeds, the woman then changes her leading zone for the future sexual activity.*

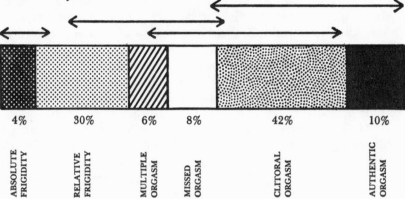

*Spectrum of Feminine Erotic Response*
This spectrum has been estimated as an approximate breakdown of 100 percent. The arrows indicate the range of possible shift, either spontaneously or with treatment. There is a range of responses within each woman, depending on the processing of the variables for each sexual engagement. But as indicated above, there is a limit to the range of shift.

As one imagines a rather stubborn clitoris refusing Dr. Freud's urgent commands, one cannot help wondering how such a small organ managed to attain such a strong independent volition. My own appendix was unreasonably strong-willed until it was finally excised, but then everyone knows that an appendix is notoriously stubborn.

Be that as it may, Dr. Shainess has this to say about Freud's clitoral analysis: "While I have abandoned many of Freud's theoretical concepts, let me bow in the direction of his superb understanding of feminine sexual mechanics—with the clarification that I do not think he meant that the clitoris had to give up its *total* excitability, but rather, its major role in the genital experience." She then goes on to comment on other theoretical approaches to this same subject:

*Masters and Johnson gave great impetus to the idea of a single major erotic site in women as there is in men—in this case, the clitoris. I attribute this to the fact that an orgasm can occur from purely clitoral stimulation, and that for their purposes, they made no distinction between masturbation and intercourse in women, in point of fact, expressing their* preference *for masturbation. In effect, they were telling Little Red Riding Hood "All the better to see you, my dear." This elimination of the vaginal, or some equivalent of it, simplified matters—for the doctor, the research subject, the psychoanalyst, and the problematic patient or nonpatient. . . . It is interesting to observe that many of the more militant feminists found this single clitoral response pleasing. It resulted in the now well-known paper by Anne Koedt called "The Myth of Vaginal Orgasm"; and Ti-Grace Atkinson called the vaginal orgasm a "mass hysterical survival response." (I interpret this as meaning that women give men what they want to believe sexually, in order to survive socially.) It also made lesbian activity seem more "natural."*

When ones notes that Dr. Shainess herself makes an unequivocal value judgment in saying that the vaginal orgasm is the "authentic orgasm" (see foregoing graph), one soon realizes that the vaginal-versus-clitoral controversy is often more adversary than scientific, that the reasoning of the various parties is often impelled by a prior bias, moral or otherwise.

## RESPONSE TO CUNNILINGUS

Bearing in mind the emotional complexity of the vaginal-clitoral debate, one might well expect an even greater tangle of psychic conflicts concerning the oral stimulation of the female genitals, which bears the quaint Latin label of *cunnilingus*. Many women (at least 50 percent of the respondents in this survey) desire or are at least curious about this type of sexual activity; but a vast majority would hesitate to ask their husbands or lovers to accommodate them—even though most of them having willingly accommodated their menfolk (or satisfied their own wishes) by performing oral sex on their genitals. Perhaps this hesitancy is due to their awareness that for most men the term "cocksucker" is the ultimate insult, as can be seen by graffiti in thousands of public restrooms throughout the country and probably in every other country where bathroom art is in vogue. There is also the element of presumed "male submission" when cunnilingus is performed, which may be inferred from the term "going down on me."

Here, again, my study showed only a slight difference in the comparative percentage of Jewish and gentile women who have experienced cunnilingus, 15 percent to 12 percent, respectively. A random sample of comments by those who *have* (and also those who *have not*) casts a revealing light on the emotional response to this aspect of sexual behavior:

"As much as I like to experiment with sex—like screwing underwater and things like that—I wouldn't dare to ask Billy to go down on me. He'd probably slap me—or even walk out on me. But I'd still like to try it. I mean if he would do it on his own. I've even dreamed that he's doing it to me."

"To paraphrase that old proverb, honey, you can lead a man to pussy, but you can't make him eat it."

"After reading Masters and Johnson and two or three other sex books, my husband and I thought we might try cunnilingus. But then we got into this long discussion about it, I mean from all angles, with Stanley analyzing the pros and cons like some damned Talmudic scholar. And after a while, we talked ourselves out of wanting sex of any kind—at least for that night. I keep wondering if gentiles ever talk themselves into a sexual impasse, or if this is mostly a Jewish trait. I sometimes wish that Stanley and I could do less thinking and more *doing*. On the other hand, all this talking may be his way of escaping sex itself."

"I've been sort of curious about it, but I don't think I'd want my lover to go down on me. He would seem . . . I don't know, sort of different if he did. But I wouldn't mind some stranger doing it to me—I mean someone I'm not emotionally tied to."

"I don't think there's complete love if a man won't kiss you the way you kiss him. Like when I'm doing it to him, I feel a fantastic closeness to him, especially when he starts to moan and squirm. So why shouldn't he want to please me the same way? Love has got to be mutual."

"Maybe I smell bad down there, even when I douche and use lots of deodorant spray. Anyway, I wouldn't want him to think I'm not clean."

"Men are a lot more uptight about sex than women are. Like for instance, I like to put his thing in my mouth and feel him getting all excited and ready to come, but I guess most men don't feel the same way—at least not the ones I've met."

While interviewing my 722 subjects, I detected a certain restraint (often outright reluctance) when the subject of oral clitoral stimulation was broached. Shere Hite noted a similar reaction in her survey:

*Remember how beautiful and enthusiastic the language was that was used to describe intercourse and general arousal? But notice how spare and tight, unenthusiastic and secretive the language has become here. Obviously women do not feel proud about clitoral stimulation in any form. Our culture has discouraged clitoral stimulation, even to the point of not giving it a name. "Cunnilingus" at least is a name, even if its meaning is not clear to everyone, but "manual clitoral stimulation" is just a phrase that is used to describe an activity that has no name. Our language for, as well as our respect for, clitoral stimulation is almost nonexistent. Our culture is still a long way from understanding, not to mention celebrating, female sexuality.*

## INTERCOURSE WITH MALES _____

With respect to conventional intercourse, my data suggest that Jewish adult females are more active sexually than gentile females, especially after they have emerged from their tease-but-don't-fornicate phase. I base this conclusion on the answers I got from a series of questions relating to frequency of intercourse with a male partner. My five arbitrarily selected categories were: Frequent (several times per week), Moderate (once a week), Minimal (once or twice per month), Infrequent (a few times per year) and None.

|  | Frequent | Moderate | Minimal | Infrequent | None |
|---|---|---|---|---|---|
| *Jewish Women* |  |  |  |  |  |
| Age 20–30 | 28% | 40% | 18% | 4% | 10% |
| Age 31–40 | 10 | 38 | 32 | 12 | 8 |
| Age 41–60 | 6 | 36 | 26 | 18 | 14 |
| Age 60 plus | 1 | 10 | 14 | 29 | 46 |
| *Gentile Women* |  |  |  |  |  |
| Age 20–30 | 24% | 34% | 26% | 6% | 10% |
| Age 31–40 | 8 | 32 | 40 | 12 | 8 |
| Age 41–60 | 3 | 28 | 32 | 25 | 12 |
| Age 60 plus | 1 | 8 | 20 | 25 | 46 |

There are, of course, many different ways of performing intercourse, but almost 75 percent of our respondents usually groove into one or two positions and seldom vary. Indeed, most women (about 64 percent) seemed to prefer what is generally known as the "missionary" or face-to-face position, but there is strong evidence that most of those 64 percent might prefer some variation if their male partners were so inclined. It is interesting to note that more gentile women regularly have missionary sex (60%) than do Jewish women (45%), but this differential may simply reflect the preference of their masculine partners rather than their own. Within the gentile group there are also some differences, with WASP females far outnumbering Catholic females in adhering to the missionary technique. My sample included the wives of two rabbis, both of whom said they hadn't had missionary sex since early in their marriages. The wife of a Protestant minister, on the other hand, admitted, "I wouldn't know what to do in any other position."

There are also some striking differences between gentiles and Jews with respect to intercourse during menstruation. About 20 percent of the gentile women have sex during their menstrual period, as compared with 25 percent of the Jewish women we interviewed. That 5 percent difference becomes more significant when one considers the total abstinence of Orthodox Jewish women during menstruation, thus clearly indicating that Conservative and Reform Jews are far more liberated from this ancient taboo than the average gentile.

As for "pretended orgasm" during intercourse, which Masters and Johnson regard as counterproductive and psychologically harmful, there is once again a disparity along ethnic lines. For example, 70 percent of Jewish women regularly deceive their husbands in this way, often claiming ecstatic orgasms to match their partner's moment of climax. Gentile women, perhaps not given to sexual theatrics, are less apt to employ this ploy. Only 55 percent admit to pretended orgasm, but that statistic may be skewed by the fact that New England and Midwestern WASP females seem perhaps puritanically incapable of deceiving their lovers or husbands during that moment of truth. Catholic women seem less bound by such truth compulsions, which leads one to wonder how often a priest might hear a female parishioner shyly confess that "I sort of lied to my husband during this very important moment."

## ADULTERY

With respect to adultery, Jewish women once again register a higher percentage than their gentile sisters—40 percent as opposed to 30 percent. But that 8-to-6 ratio decreases to about 1 to 1 for college-educated females married to professionals (doctors, lawyers and such) and businessmen, which would suggest that socioeconomic status is a more important factor in adultery than ethnic background. (Slightly less than 75 percent of Jewish and gentile graduates have engaged in adulterous affairs at least once.) In other words, a Wellesley graduate of any race who is married to a lawyer is much more apt to commit adultery than a high-school graduate married to a garbage collector— probably because the high schooler has less free time and less mobility, and because her working-class husband might react more violently to being a cuckold than a lawyer would.

Consequently, the aforementioned 8-to-6 ratio may merely reflect the fact that Jewish women tend to be better educated and better off economically than gentile women, rather than having a more promiscuous nature. For both groups, adultery occurs more frequently between the ages of thirty and forty, with a gradual decrease between forty-one and fifty, and a sharp decrease after that. Only two women in my survey, both gentiles, admitted adulterous conduct after the age of sixty; one of them is married to a psychoanalyst and the other to a mortician.

The following comments from respondents provide some fascinating clues to feminine attitudes about sexual intercourse, adulterous or otherwise:

"I get so bored with the so-called missionary position—always face to face with my husband. It wouldn't be so bad, I guess, if he wouldn't slobber and spit in my face as he's beginning to come. Which I never do."

"In my book, Jews are the best lovers, they're generally pretty considerate and sort of humorous, you know. And they like to try different positions, not just face to face. There was this one guy, some kind of teacher, who used to drive me wild with the scissor lock. That's what he called it—'my scissor lock.' He claimed it gave him more traction—whatever that is."

"My first ex-husband liked to come in from behind, which was okay by me, except that he would sometimes wiggle and shift around so much that it felt like I had some kinda monkey on my back. And that would distract me."

"My husband won't even touch me when I'm menstruating, which is really frustrating, because that's when I really start craving for sex. I once tried to approach him during my period, and he almost shoved me off the bed. 'Come off that crap,' he said, 'I don't want all that damned blood on me.' So now I stay away from him, and just play with myself to get rid of that crazy urge."

"Several years ago I met this French guy, who was the only man that ever screwed me while I was riding the red pony. That's what we called our period back in high school—riding the red pony. Anyway, this French guy said he liked sex a lot more when a woman's bleeding—and I think he really meant it."

"My lover gets turned off when I've got my period. And, quite frankly, I wouldn't want anyone to touch me when I'm that way. It seems sort of not healthy."

"Sure, I've pretended to have orgasms. You've got to, honey, otherwise your man is gonna think he's not good enough to make you come. So you just fake a little and keep his ego straight."

"Since I never have an orgasm with just plain intercourse, I have to fake it to make him think he's really satisfied me. That's because he never plays with my . . . well, at least not enough to make me come. So I've got to do that part by myself—and never let him know that I do it."

"I don't know of any woman who *doesn't* pretend that she's coming, at least once in a while. Like you don't really feel like a real woman if you don't come. At least he won't think so."

"You're supposed to come—at the same time he does—so you have to fake it. And I'm a great faker."

"After those first few years, when the honeymoon was really over, I started looking around for something new, and I guess the tennis club was about the best place to look. It somehow seems more socially acceptable. It's not like hanging around some bar, hoping to be picked up and laid by just anyone who comes along. I mean you can be more selective at a tennis club."

"When I have an outside affair, I want it to be low-down and dirty. Like my husband when he picks up a whore."

"The only times I've cheated was with my husband's best friends."

"Most of the fun, for me at least, is having a secret lover. It's like living two lives under one roof."

"I had this one lover who liked to have me when I was menstruating, and after we'd come he would rub the blood around the sheets like some kid fingerpainting. He would make these strange patterns that looked like Rorschach blots. Anyway, it made me a lot less self-conscious about having my period. It was like celebrating my condition."

"I'd feel a lot better if I knew my husband was also having affairs. That way it would be even-Steven, which happens to be his name."

"I'm sure we both know that we're cheating, but we never talk about it."

"So often, especially when Jerome is off on a long business trip, I get this aching feeling in my womb, a sort of overwhelming emptiness, as if I need someone to fill that awful void—to make me feel whole again."

This last comment brings to mind a uniquely feminine sensation which Shere Hite has described in considerable detail in her report on female sexuality:

*There is a very specific but important question that has been saved until last, something that will be referred to throughout this book as the phenomenon of "vaginal ache," that is often perceived as the desire for vaginal penetration. It is part of the same question just discussed, i.e., the difference in feeling between orgasm with intercourse or without. This feeling of intense desire, or "ache" (desire to be filled), comes during the buildup to orgasm, very near the moment of orgasm itself, and then spills over into the orgasmic contractions.*

*What happens is this: sometimes building up to and just at the moment of orgasm there is an intense pleasure/pain feeling deep inside the vagina, something like a desire to be entered or touched inside, or just an exquisite sensation of pleasure, which we call "vaginal ache." It is an almost hollow feeling, and is caused because the upper end, the deeper portion, of the vagina is ballooning out, expanding into what has theoretically been pictured as a little lake for the collection and holding of semen.*

*Some women perceive this feeling as hollow, empty, and unpleasant, while others find it intensely pleasurable. Whether you prefer to have a penis there or not at that moment depends on your own personal preference, of course. For most women, "vaginal ache" is not felt so intensely with a penis present; the penis seems to "soothe" and diffuse the feeling, so it depends on whether you prefer to feel the sensation or not.*

## LESBIAN RELATIONSHIPS _____

Alfred Kinsey once estimated that perhaps 12 to 13 percent of American women had "sexual relations to the point of orgasm" with another female at some time during their adult lives, and that between 11 and 20 percent of single women and 8 to 10 percent of married women in his nationwide survey "were making at least incidental homosexual responses, or making more specific homosexual contacts" between the ages of twenty and thirty-five. In a more recent study, Shere Hite reported that 8 percent of her female respondents preferred sex with women, while an additional 9 percent identified themselves as "bisexual." Moreover, about 3 percent preferred to have sex with themselves.

My numerical calculations yield a figure halfway between Kinsey's and Hite's, with about 14 percent of female interviewees reporting at least one lesbian relationship in their adult years. Within this overall percentage, there seems to be a three-point spread between Jewish and gentile females, but, here again, the differential may merely reflect the Jewish women's greater willingness to talk about their sex lives, particularly in matters which might seem abnormal or immoral. Another reason may be the preponderance of Jewish women in the comparatively recent feminist movements, some sectors of which emphasize independence from men. Dr. Richard Green, formerly associated with the UCLA Gender Identity Research Treatment Program, has predicted an increase in bisexuality and/or lesbianism among women "partly for political reasons"—as one of many ways for women to "disassociate themselves from the extraordinary dependency they've had on men all these years."

Referring to Kinsey's insistence that the world "is a continuum in each and every one of its aspects" and that homosexuality and heterosexuality are only the extremes of "a rich and varied continuum," Hite suggests that "lesbian," "homosexual" and "heterosexual" should be used as adjectives rather than nouns. In others words, "*people* are not properly described as homosexuals, lesbians or heterosexual"; rather their *activities* should be so described. Whatever words they use to describe themselves or their behavior, women engaged in lesbian activity express a wide variety of attitudes, from nonchalant pride to ill-disguised guilt:

"Now that I've come out, I realize that men are just excess baggage. I get all the sex I need from my sisters—or from myself."
"There's no man who can satisfy a woman the way another

woman can. Only a woman's delicate hands and lips can stimulate your clit the way it ought to be. Men are brutes."

"My friend Nina and I spent many nights together at high-school slumber parties. We'd snuggle up to each other and maybe kiss a little—nothing passionate or anything like that. Just light little kisses, which didn't mean anything. But about five years after our double wedding to the Hansen twins, Nina and I got our husbands to take us to Acapulco. Anyway, we went swimming one afternoon, and, suddenly, while we were horsing around in these big waves, Nina and I started wrestling and hugging and kissing each other—like when we were kids. Then all of a sudden Ron came splashing over and pulled Nina away from me and started calling me a goddamned lesbian."

"Okay, I'll tell you why I'm bisexual. It's because I married this square who would never go down on me—wouldn't even consider it. Then I met this fantastic woman who showed me what sex really was. So that's why."

"Well, to tell you the truth, I've had two or three incidents with women, and I really enjoyed them. But afterwards—I mean, when my husband and I were in bed together—I would get these awful guilt feelings, and I'd feel sort of dirty and perverted and really sick about it."

"I had my first lesbian experience with this Italian woman who taught a pottery class in the Catskills one summer. When she first went down on me, she kept raving about how much she loved *cunnilinguini*. Then she would always say, 'It sure is better than *fellatochini*.' And when she explained that last word to me, I almost died laughing. I guess sex was just like food to Rosalina, and she really had a huge appetite."

## USE OF DILDOS, VIBRATORS AND OTHER MECHANICAL DEVICES

Although there seems to be a marked increase in the use of dildos, vibrators and other mechanical substitutes for the male penis, only a very few women are willing to admit that they use them. And if such objects are used, they are carefully hidden from husbands, lovers or even casual male visitors. As one woman told me, "My friend Irma has a vibrator, but she hides it in the laundry hamper, where her husband never looks. But if he ever found it, I think he'd kill her—because that would be telling him that his thing isn't good enough." Another woman said that *her* friend had an ebony-colored vibrator on which she had inscribed the name of her former black lover. Still another woman reported that "judging from the women I've known, I'd guess that at least forty percent of American women use vibrators or something similar—like bottles or some other object."

That percentage seems inordinately high, but there is no way to make an accurate estimation. Suffice it to say that many more women use such devices than are willing to admit they do. Note, for example, that two of my aforementioned informants referred to "friends" who used vibrators, which is a familiar ploy to avoid reference to oneself. Considering the average male's overt or inchoate fear of sexual inadequacy (particularly in middle age), one can well understand why women studiously conceal such objects in out-of-the-way hiding places which their menfolk usually ignore, such as laundry hampers, linen closets, sewing kits, old handbags, Tampax boxes or such. One very resourceful woman hides her plastic dildo (nicknamed for a famous macho novelist) inside the hollow head that holds her favorite wig.

Since it is probably impossible to ascertain whether 5, 10 or 40 percent use an artificial phallus to satisfy erotic needs, it is equally difficult to discern any difference between Jewish and gentile women in this particular sexual practice. But my data do suggest that women between thirty and fifty years of age are twice as likely to use these devices as women under the age of thirty. It is also evident that single or divorced women, particularly those from the middle class, are more apt to use them than poorer married women. Among the few women willing to discuss this subject came comments like the following:

"I got mine from this Italian boyfriend. He was going on a business trip for four or five days and he brought me this flesh-colored vibrator in a velvet case. 'This is Butch,' he said, handing it to me with a big grin. 'I want you to use this when I'm away, so you won't miss me too much. But, remember, Debby, no one but Butch.' Well, let me tell you, as one of your typical Jewish princesses, I've gotten some terrific gifts in my time—but nothing like Vito's."

"This may sound too liberated to you—but I like to use my vibrator on my clit during intercourse. And if some man can't take that scene, I just say 'fuck him' and find someone who can."

"Sometimes a dildo comes in pretty handy. Like this friend of mine was about to get raped, and she bashed his head with her dildo, just like you'd use a blackjack."

## STREET LANGUAGE IN THE BEDROOM

In recent years, according to many sexologists, there has been a marked increase in the use of so-called "street language" in the bedroom, with both men and women referring to their genitals in words once considered verboten in mixed company. Some of this linguistic liberation can be attributed to the youth rebellion of the sixties, during which the word "fuck" (with all its various conjugations) became as common as "damn." During World War II, "fucking" had become the universal adjective and adverb among soldiers and sailors of every rank, but it was strictly confined to intramale conversations—so much so that Norman Mailer and James Jones were compelled to soften it to "friggin" to make it acceptable to squeamish book publishers. Now, less than thirty years later, junior-high-school girls pronounce it with biting clarity and monotonous regularity. Small wonder that such words have become almost *de rigueur* for certain lovers, particularly in the throes of climactic copulation, where the short, pithy words ("cunt," "cock" and "fuck") are like the gasps and sputters of overheated pistons in a machine churning for top speed.

For many men and women such words serve as audioaphrodisiacs, perhaps because certain men are turned on by what they regard as whore language, and because many women can thus momentarily indulge in a secret desire to be whores. Some psychologists might consider such earthy expletives as veiled aggression, while others might see them as nothing more than exuberant expressions of uninhibited passion and love.

Whatever their reasons, Jewish women are more apt to use sexy talk than are gentile women—but this could easily be attributed to a greater verbal facility and more experimental attitudes. My data also indicate that college-educated, middle-class women use more bawdy language than less-educated and less economically secure women, all of which may further explain the aforementioned difference between Jewish and gentile women. It should further be noted that a lawyer or doctor would be more likely to tolerate "dirty talk" from his wife than would a butcher or ditch digger, this despite the fact that working-class males themselves generally use bawdier language than middle- or upper-class professionals. Here again we see an example of *class* distinction rather than *ethnic* distinction, some of which is evident in the following comments from some female interviewees:

"I once asked my husband if he liked my thing, using that other word for it—and he almost split my head open with a hand chop. 'That's a fuckin' whore word,' he yelled. 'Don't ever say that again!' But I know that he and the guys he works with on construction, they say that word all the time when some girl passes by the job. And yet when I use it, he blows his stack, I mean really. Anyway, when I said it—just that one night—he wouldn't touch me for a week."

"Well, after Max and I saw *Carnal Knowledge* and some of the really sexy movies, we started using those words in bed, and they really turn you on."

"I like to hear my husband say them, but I couldn't say them myself."

## PORNOGRAPHIC FILMS AND LITERATURE

In recent years—particularly since the day Jacqueline Onassis was photographed leaving a much-publicized pornographic film titled *I Am Curious—Yellow*—more and more women have seen such films or read hard-core pornographic books or magazines like *Screw*. But my data indicate that the percentage of women who have attended more than one porn film is still quite low, perhaps less than 15 percent. Once again, because of the relatively rare participation in this type of activity, we were unable to detect any measurable difference between gentile and Jewish women. As one respondent summarized it, "Even sex can be boring when everything is revealed and endlessly repeated, but I guess some people are turned on by that sort of thing."

## WOMEN AND DOCTORS

An important aspect of a woman's sexuality is her relationship to the medical profession. Most women probably trust their gynecologists, but it is a mistaken trust, in the opinion of many feminists. Gena Correa, author of *The Hidden Malpractice*, spent two years researching the subject and finally concluded that men ought to be barred from obstetrics and gynecology. "This may sound radical," she says, "but that's because we're used to men. Yet they haven't always been involved in obstetrics."

Along with most proponents of natural childbirth, Correa maintains that the birth of children is much less complicated than doctors lead patients to believe—and less complicated than doctors themselves make it. She also asserts that a woman's body is not as complicated or mysterious as doctors pretend it is, and that most female surgery is totally unnecessary. After working for two years as a nurse's aide at the Peter Bent Brigham Hospital in Boston, Correa did extensive research on the medical treatment of women, studying the history of female medicine, gathering reams of statistics and information on current practice and interviewing scores of physicians, nurses and patients. And as a result of her studies, she set down certain conclusions that seem startling but which come as no surprise to the more candid members of the medical profession.

- Doctors commonly have performed sterilization on poor Spanish-speaking, black and Indian women without telling them that the operation was permanent or irreversible, or that there were other types of contraception available. Sometimes, they simply did not tell them what operation they had performed.

- Hysterectomies were the most frequently performed operation in the U.S. last year, and a good many of them were not immediately necessary. Doctors often performed them for "tipped uteri," a condition in which the uterus is tilted slightly backward, and is neither uncommon nor, in most cases, dangerous to the woman's health.

- Prophylactic hysterectomies are being performed at an alarming rate. Doctors are recommending that a woman have a hysterectomy automatically after her last "planned" child. Yet hysterectomies have a 35 to 50 percent complication rate, are extremely traumatic for most women and require four to six weeks' recovery. Furthermore, the risk of death from the operation is higher than that from cancer for women on the Pill.

- The prone position for childbirth, developed by a male doctor, makes delivery more difficult than a sitting position because a woman is delivering "uphill." The use of forceps, anesthesia because of a difficult delivery, and a greater number of Caesarean operations accompanies births in this position. These "mechanical aids," according to Correa, are often unnecessary and are even dangerous to the child, as well as to the mother.

- Eighty percent of contraception researchers are male—and most contraceptives are for women, Correa says. A "male Pill" has been possible for years, she maintains, but doctors are afraid to experiment because of possible side effects. Yet the side effects would be the same as those experienced by women on the Pill, which is still on the market.

Correa also points out that the Pill was approved for women by the Food and Drug Administration on the basis of a study which involved only 132 women who had taken it for more than one year and 718 who had taken the drug for less than one year. Five of the women died during the testing period, three with symptoms suggesting the presence of bloodclots. Since no autopsies were performed on these women, their deaths could not be conclusively attributed to the Pill—but Correa and others feel that the FDA was remiss in not insisting on autopsies before approving the drug for general use. "It's all there on the transcripts of the Senate hearings on the Pill," says Correa. "I wish women would read those manuscripts and also the transcripts on the hearings for the IUD, DES, and depo provera."

# 3
# The Sexual
# Behavior
# of Adult Males

*The man who shops from woman to woman, though his heart aches with idealism, with the desire for pure love, has entered the female realm.*

—Saul Bellow in *Time* magazine

Commenting on Saul Bellow's rather embittered belief that most women are perpetually shopping for the unattainable "one true love," a *Time* magazine critic recently implied that Bellow's long-held suspicion of women is rooted in his Orthodox religious training. Although married four times (rivaling Norman Mailer in this respect), Bellow apparently clings to the conviction that shopping is a female game, implying that when men shop around they are simply adopting a woman's *modus vivendi*. Many men, including some of Bellow's celebrated protagonists, do indeed go from one woman to another, at times desperately hoping for a lasting relationship and occasionally convincing themselves that they have finally found it. No doubt, it was this yearning that Bellow had in mind when he talked about the man whose "heart aches with idealism, with the desire for pure love."

But a friend of mine literally snorted when she read his comment. "That's the kind of soulful crap you get from a Jewish Prince when he's trying to get you into the sack. He's really convinced that a suffering heart is an irresistible aphrodisiac. Now gentiles are just as bad, mind you, except they're not so clever about it. They haven't had the long practice of suffering that we Jews have. And I guess some gentiles are more uptight about showing their feelings—even phoney ones."

59

Her cynical appraisal of the so-called Jewish Prince conforms with similar comments by many of our Jewish female interviewees, one of whom complained that her lover couldn't decide whether to be proud or vulnerable, "so he's compromised by becoming an arrogant sufferer." But a comfortable majority (74%) still prefer Jewish men, particularly as husbands. Interestingly enough, many of the 240 gentile women in this survey (34% of whom had had affairs with Jews) expressed a similar preference:

"Sure he's a prince, and he makes a lot more demands than he should. But he's also very funny and tender and surprisingly tolerant when I'm bitchy. But I wish he'd wash the dishes just once!"

"When I first met Aaron, I could see that I was just another shiksa to him—someone to amuse and abuse. But after a while, when I finally managed to penetrate his thick arrogant façade, I realized that he could be warm and loving and very amusing. I could also see that he was extremely vulnerable, which made him all the more appealing—although, now and then, he could still be the worst bastard I've ever known. But I guess I'm drawn to charming bastards, because when Aaron left I found another one just like him—then one after that. All of them Jews and all of them tender and affectionate and funny and periodically mean as hell."

"What else can you expect from a man who's been raised by a mother like his, who made him think his poopie was perfume, I'm just surprised (and, believe me, grateful) that he's no worse than he is. And sometimes he can be the sweetest, most gentle guy I know. As for sex, I can only say that even his kvetchy mother would be proud."

"As a Catholic married to a Jewish dentist who was an only child, I'd been warned (mostly by Jewish women) about the so-called Jewish Prince. Well, first of all, Stan is a lot less of a prince than my brother Sean, who is still a bachelor because he's never met anyone good enough for him. On the other hand, Stan is such a fantastic guy that all my gentile girl friends want me to find them Jewish husbands . . . and not necessarily dentists or doctors."

"I'm told that women with alcoholic fathers often marry alcoholic husbands. Well, I got the same kind of problem: my father was a born sufferer, so I went and married another born sufferer. And right now I'm wishing someone would organize a Sufferers Anonymous, so that my husband could go somewhere and share his grief with someone other than me. I've never known anyone with such a capacity for gloom. He even makes jokes about his hard luck, but when you get through laughing, you're even sadder than before. Sometimes I wish I'd married an arrogant show-off like my sister Becky married."

In determining whether Jews are better husbands and/or lovers than gentiles, we might profitably analyze their overall behavior in matters relating to sex. With this in mind, we shall explore their range of sexual activity and attitudes with respect to breast envy, petting to climax, masturbation, fantasies and nocturnal emissions, intercourse with females, oral sex with females, response to fellatio by female partners, clitoral or vaginal stimulation of partner, other types of foreplay, use of bawdy language during intercourse, reaction to pornographic films and literature, homosexual relationships, the virgin-mother complex, attitudes toward stepchildren, sado-masochism and contact with animals.

## BREAST ENVY

Having seen that male infants and young children have an obsession about female breasts (Chapter 1), it is not at all surprising to learn that most males continue to be obsessed with bosoms throughout their adult lives. One needs no further evidence than the enormous success of such magazines as *Playboy*, *Hustler* and the earlier *Esquire*, all of which have raised the female breast to the sanctity of the most ancient totems. Indeed, some future anthropologist or historian is likely to name this period "the great mammary age," when a certain pale-faced guru named Hugh Hefner led millions of worshippers and cultists, whose solemn and only prayer was "the bigger the better."

More than 98 percent of my male subjects consider breasts a major erogenous zone, the others being the pelvic region, buttocks and legs. When asked to rank these four parts of the female anatomy on a scale of one to four, our male interviewees responded as follows:

|  | First | Second | Third | Fourth |
|---|---|---|---|---|
| Breasts | 54% | 32% | 12% | 0% |
| Pelvis | 32 | 34 | 38 | 2 |
| Buttocks | 20 | 29 | 38 | 10 |
| Legs | 3 | 4 | 10 | 14 |
| Other | 1 | 1 | 2 | 7 |

There are, of course, certain men whose preferences vary from the norm. For example, about .3 percent are foot fetishists, about .2 percent are mainly interested in nostrils and one respondent, who is "turned off by any kind of tits," has only one erotic interest: double chins on red-haired women. Perhaps assuming that their visual preferences are an accurate clue to how women feel about their own bodies, most breast lovers erroneously confine their foreplay to fondling or nibbling nipples, when, in fact, their bedmates probably prefer clitoral or vaginal stimulation.

With respect to ethnic inclinations, my data show that of the 54 percent who give first rank to breasts, 60 percent are Jewish and 40 percent are gentiles. But there is no ethnic differential among those who make the pelvis their first choice. As for those who rank buttocks as *numero uno*, about 66 percent are gentiles and 33 percent are Jewish. The 66 percent reflects a very marked preference for buttocks by gentiles of Latin extraction. One should note that *Latinos* are equally partial to large breasts. This can be easily explained when one considers the close resemblance between buttocks and bosoms. In fact, the buttocks can be regarded—in a visual sense—as blown-up versions of the female breasts. Would it be too farfetched to assume that homosexual men who wear tight-fitting trousers are merely flaunting their surrogate bosoms? (It is interesting to note in this regard that most Mexican and other *Latino* males literally worship their mothers. More about this when we discuss the virgin-mother complex.)

The ramifications of the breast obsession can be seen in numerous symbolic references. Take, for example, the old mountain climber whose young robust son needlingly challenged him to climb a towering peak. "Come on, Dad," he said, "I'll beat you to the top of that big tit."

Though seemingly novel, that analogy is probably as old as recorded history, certainly as old as the ancient Aztec empire, during which a certain section of a mountain range was called "the sleeping lady" because its two most prominent volcanic peaks resembled a female bosom. In the piquant *nahuatl* language of the Aztecs, one of the peaks was called *ixtacihuatl*, which translates into "frozen nipple." The other was called *popocatepetl*, which in gross vernacular means "icy teat." One should also note that the natives of Tanzania refer to Mount Kilimanjaro as "the giant breast," a bit of local folklore which somehow escaped the attention of the usually knowledgeable

Ernest Hemingway. Perhaps he was unconsciously repressing his own well-publicized obsession with that part of the female anatomy. As one of his old friends recently commented, "Ernie was always a boob-and-fanny lover; that's why he liked living in Cuba."

The mountain-breast analogy is also frequently used by the natives of Tibet, one of whom once proudly boasted to Sir Edmund Hillary that "we are surrounded by beautiful breasts, but that one [pointing to Mount Everest] belongs to the single-breast goddess who guides our destiny." To which Hillary reportedly replied, "I need only my mother's blessing." In this respect, one might profitably speculate on why most mountain climbers (certainly those born in occidental cultures) have inordinately close ties to their mothers. I recently interviewed seventy-six members of a college mountain-climbing club, asking that they respond to a questionnaire dealing with sexual and familial attitudes, and we subsequently determined that more than 80 percent showed clear evidence of pronounced mother fixation.

But the mountain-breast syndrome is not entirely unique. There are countless comparisons between other objects and female breasts. For example, the Taj Mahal has been irreverently dubbed "the bloated marble teat" by the low-paid workmen who daily clean the pool that reflects that glorious mausoleum built in 1630–52 by the Shah Jahan for his wife. The groundskeepers of the state Capitol in Denver, Colorado, are equally earthy when they refer to the Capitol dome as "the golden tit."

Indeed, as one reflects upon the nippled domes that grace the Capitol buildings of almost every state and the pervasive use of domelike or semicircular motifs in architectural designs, one could easily argue that we live in a breast-worshipping society. And as Li Po once remarked, "We worship only what we fear or envy."

## RANGE OF SEXUAL ACTIVITY

Although petting to climax is usually associated with high-school and college students who resist "going all the way" for various reasons, there is a small but significant percentage of adult males who have orgasms without intercourse. About 27 percent of my interviewees admit having this kind of sexual climax on several occasions—some quite frequently—and within this group 55 percent are Jewish and 45 percent are gentiles, most of whom are Catholic. (One should, of course, distinguish between this type of orgasm and *coitus interruptus*, which represents a more intense degree of frustration as well as a remarkable sense of restraint.) According to some of my interviews, the Jewish-gentile differential may be caused by the previously discussed tease-but-don't-capitulate tactics of young Jewish women. The same would be true of young Catholic women, for whom fornication is only slightly less sinful than adultery. Following are a few comments, culled from my files, which bear upon this aspect of sexual behavior:

"I dated this Catholic nurse for almost three years, probably the most beautiful shiksa I ever knew, but we never actually screwed. I mean she let me do everything but that, and, of course, I would always end up creaming my goddamned pants. I tell ya, my cleaning bills were astronomical with that chick. But, you know, I had a lot more satisfaction with her than with a lotta chicks I actually laid. With her, it was like having a virgin every time we got together—only we never got together."

"There was this one little princess who really drove me crazy. She would get me all hot and bothered with a lot of sexy talk and she'd rub her crotch against mine as if she really meant to go all the way this time, rolling her tongue in my ear and giving me the damndest French kisses I ever had—and finally she'd make me come without ever letting me get where I wanted. It was sheer agony and I really hated getting that goo all over my shorts, my shirttails and my damned slacks. Then I'd have to worry if my wife would notice that dried-up stuff on my clothes."

"There's nothing like creaming your pants to make you feel like a teenager again. I really hate that crap, but there's this girl who works for me, who will neck like hell with me—just about everything you can imagine—but I always end up coming in my damned handkerchief or all over the back seat of my car. Now that's really teenage stuff, but what are you going to do? You take what comes and you're grateful. Anyway, it's better than wanging your own dong."

"Lately, I meet nothing but teasers. Some gal gives you a big come-on at some bar, and a couple of hours later you're outside her doorway, necking like a goddamn teenager and finally soaking your pants with all that messy goo. At my age—look, I'm pushing fifty—I should know better. I keep telling myself, 'Settle down, find someone your own age,' but every weekend I'm back at the same damn bar, thinking this time I'll really score."

As Dr. Kinsey noted more than thirty years ago, the frequency of petting to climax varies considerably between males of different educational levels. In the later teens, this source provides nearly three times more orgasms for males who attend college. Between the ages of twenty-one and twenty-five, there are five times as many orgasms from petting for college men as there are for males who never go beyond grade school. The less-educated males derive from 1 to 2 percent of their total orgasmic outlet from petting in premarital years, whereas college males derive 5 to 8 percent of their total outlet from necking. Our data also confirm Kinsey's finding that petting is most characteristic of the upper socioeconomic levels. Consequently, the aforementioned differences between Jews and gentiles are due more to social factors than to ethnic inclinations.

## MASTURBATION AND ANXIETY

Not surprisingly, the above-mentioned socioeconomic behavioral patterns prevail with respect to masturbation by adult males. My data once again affirm Kinsey's report that differences in frequency of masturbation at different educational levels is most striking among married males of all ethnic groups. At the grade-school level, there are only 20 to 30 percent who regularly masturbate, with the accumulative incidence figures rising only a bit during the later years of marriage. The high-school graduates follow the same pattern, but among college-educated men, 60 to 70 percent regularly masturbate in each of the periods cited above. Moreover, within the grade-school group, only 1 to 3 percent get their total orgasmic outlet through this activity, whereas 8.5 to 10 percent of college graduates attain their total output in this way, and that percentage rises to 20 percent in the later years of marriage.

Here again, we note a difference between Jewish and gentile men (73% to 67%), which no doubt reflects the higher educational achievement of Jews. Interestingly enough, college-educated WASPs apparently have a higher frequency of masturbation than either Jews or Catholics. Since self-stimulation is an inherently private and solitary activity, this particular differential could be attributed to a Protestant preference for privacy in all sexual matters. Certainly this is true with respect to orgies, in which Jews and Catholics participate five times more frequently than WASPs.

Although most of our male respondents were initially reluctant to discuss their own masturbatory activities, eventually they were quite candid and occasionally amusing:

"When you get to my age, your chances of finding a sex partner are pretty slim. So I just beat my meat whenever I get horny, which ain't too often these days."

"Whenever I catch my six-year-old son playing with himself, I give him that old warning I got from dad: 'It will stunt your growth.' Yet two or three times a week, I sneak up to the bathroom for a bit of old-time masturbation. But, of course, I can risk it—I'm already six feet, three inches tall."

"Well, it's a lot simpler and certainly a lot cheaper. Besides, you never get turned down by your own penis—at least not too often."

"I figure if my wife can do it, why shouldn't I? You might even say that a couple who masturbates together stays together . . . or at least *comes* together."


## FANTASIES AND NOCTURNAL EMISSIONS_____

Most sexologists agree that a high percentage of males—probably 80 to 85 percent—experience nocturnal emissions at some time in their lives. Here, again, socioeconomic status seems to be an important determinant. Over 99 percent of college-educated males have had wet dreams, but that high figure drops to 85 percent for high-school graduates and 75 percent for males who never go beyond grade school. Since they are generally more educated, Jewish males have a higher incidence of nocturnal emissions than gentiles.

Nevertheless, these so-called wet dreams constitute only a minimal portion of the total orgasmic outlet of any social group. For example, college-level males in their twenties derive about 12 to 16 percent of their total orgasms from this source; but that percentage drops to 8 percent for males with a high-school education and 6 percent for those with only a grade-school education. Among married males such emissions account for 3 to 4 percent of total outlet.

That latter figure may seem surprising at first, but not when one considers wet dreams as substitutes for actual intercourse, which is so frequently frustrated in premarital situations. Quite often, however, the actual experience of orgasm is not realized in the dream itself. Even when a man awakes to find himself ejaculating, he may not have reached the fulfillment of his desired goal within the dream. Most individuals are awakened by the orgasm, while a few go on sleeping. In any event, such dreams generally relate to one's overt daytime experience or at least a consciously desired experience. For this reason, we would like to cite a few portions of such dreams as related to us by several respondents:

"About once a month I have this dream about me and Jackie Onassis getting together on a very romantic basis. Now, I have never actually laid her—she's always resisting at the very last moment, see—but, man, I always come—I mean all over my goddamned silk sheets."

"Listen, I always know when I'm going to have one of those wet dreams. I can feel it coming just before I doze off. So I get myself a towel and shove it between my legs, which makes me feel like a true Boy Scout—always prepared."

"You can always figure when you've been out with a Jewish princess who ain't putting out, or when you see Raquel Welch shoving her crotch at you in technicolor, that you're going to cream the sheets. Right? So with me, I always hop in bed with a few sheets of Bounty paper towel and I'm all set. But, listen, it's gotta be Bounty. That's the only kind that really absorbs everything."

"For seven or eight years—maybe more—I kept having dreams about this nun who taught us at St. Joseph's High. Then I finally switched to Marilyn Monroe—which was pretty wild, man, because I was also dreaming I could hit more homers than Joe DiMaggio—and those were the wettest dreams I ever had. But after she died, I sort of dried up. Even when I tried to dream about some of those other sexpots, nothing ever happened anymore."

"Well, as you've probably guessed, I'm gay and proud of it. But I keep having these creepy heterosexual dreams, where I'm actually balling this woman at my ad agency. And it really makes me feel awfully guilty. Like I always confide everything in my lover—that's part of our thing, really confiding—but I somehow can't bring myself to tell him about these particular dreams."

Although it is probably statistically insignificant, my cumulative data suggest that when Jewish men engage in sexual fantasies, they almost always see themselves as principal participants; whereas gentiles often imagine themselves as mere observers of the focal action in their fantasies or dreams.

## INTERCOURSE WITH FEMALES

As in the case of Jewish females, my survey shows that adult Jewish males are more active sexually than gentile males, especially in what might be called "conventional sexual intercourse." I base this conclusion on the answers I got from a series of questions relating to frequency of intercourse with a female partner. Once again, my five arbitrarily selected categories were: Frequent (several times per week), Moderate (once a week), Minimal (once or twice a month), Infrequent (a few times per year) and None.

|  | Frequent | Moderate | Minimal | Infrequent | None |
|---|---|---|---|---|---|
| *Jewish Men* | | | | | |
| Age 20–30 | 36% | 39% | 15% | 2% | 8% |
| 31–40 | 18% | 40% | 27% | 10% | 5% |
| 41–60 | 10% | 38% | 24% | 18% | 10% |
| 60 plus | 2% | 12% | 10% | 20% | 56% |
| *Gentile Men* | | | | | |
| Age 20–30 | 32% | 34% | 26% | 2% | 6% |
| 31–40 | 16% | 38% | 30% | 8% | 8% |
| 41–60 | 6% | 32% | 26% | 16% | 20% |
| 60 plus | 1% | 8% | 8% | 18% | 65% |

Although there are various ways of having intercourse, almost 70 percent of my respondents usually confine themselves to one or two positions, particularly after marriage. In fact, most males (about 60 percent) seem to have a preference for the face-to-face "missionary" technique and will often get turned off if their wives should suggest, or even hint at a desire for, any variation from that ancient norm. Of the 40 percent who are willing to try a few of the legendary fifty-two positions of the Kama Sutra, 55 percent are Jewish and 45 percent are gentile. Within the gentile group, Catholics are apparently more experimental than Protestants. But even among the experimenters (of whichever ethnic group), men appear to be more inhibited than women, both physically and verbally, as one can gather from the following comments:

"Well, as I see it, your so-called missionary position was good enough for my dad and my granddad and probably a lotta generations before them. So why the hell should I be different? As long as you come good, there ain't no reason to change."

"Look, I know my old lady might like something different now and then. She's even hinted. As a matter of fact, I've done a couple of new tricks with this girl at the office—I mean like coming in from behind—but I just can't see myself doing that kinda stuff with my own wife. Now, the scissor position might be okay, but I'm not really sure."

"After you've tried the kind of things my girl and I are into, that old missionary style is for the birds. You've really got to swing from every angle—upside, downside, sideways, and catty-corner—otherwise you get into a real rut. Now don't ask me to explain about catty-cornering; it just can't be described with words. You've got to see yourself, or at least a picture of it."

"Well, first of all, I'm a Methodist minister—but, quite frankly, I've never used the missionary position."

"I'd like to do it some other way, especially when your woman sits on you and squirms like a goddamn snake. But when you've had a double inguinal hernia, you've got to settle for something more conventional. But it's sure tempting to do something different."

As one might expect, deviations from the norm often reflect the socioeconomic status of the sexual partners, with upper-class males tending to be more experimental and working-class males preferring more conventional fornication. For example, 65 percent of those who penetrate from behind (or use a scissor position) are college graduates; while 68 percent of those who usually confine themselves to the missionary technique are men with a high-school or grade-school education. Some of the latter group, à la Archie Bunker, tend to believe that "only a pervert would do it like some animal." An Italian butcher once tried to vary his angle of penetration and was scoldingly accused of being "some kind of queer" by his usually docile forty-year-old wife.

According to Kinsey, all social levels of our Anglo-American culture feel that there is one coital position which is biologically natural, and that all others are man-devised variants which are perversions. However, he goes on to say:

> [*The*] *one position which might be defended as natural because it is usual throughout the Class Mammalia, is not the one commonly used in our culture. The usual mammalian position involves, of course, rear entrance, with the female more or less prone, face down, with her legs flexed under her body, while the male is above or to the rear. . . . Most persons will be surprised to learn that positions in intercourse are as much a product of human cultures as language and clothing, and that the common English-American position is rare in some cultures. Among the several thousand portrayals of human coitus in the art left by ancient civilizations, there is hardly a single portrayal of the English-American position. It will be recalled that Malinowski (1929) records the nearly universal use of a totally different position among the Trobrianders in the Southwestern Pacific; and that he notes that caricatures of the English-American position are performed around the communal campfires, to the great amusement of the natives who refer to the position as the "missionary position."*

## THE VIRGIN-MOTHER COMPLEX

Like many Chicanos and Irish Catholics, a high percentage of Jews tend to have much less intercourse with their wives after they bear children. Dr. Helen Singer Kaplan, in her highly praised book, *The New Sex Therapy*, notes that a certain type of man "might also be rendered impotent if he experiences anxiety when attempting to have intercourse with his wife because she subtly resembles his mother." And, of course, this resemblance is reinforced when the wife does in fact become the mother of his child. For many a Catholic this problem is further compounded by an unconscious association of his own mother with the Virgin Mary, and that symbolic fusion may well be carried over to his wife. Thus, to continue to have sex with her would seem to be an incestuous violation of her neo-virginity.

Since Jews have no Virgin Mary to exacerbate their Oedipal confusions, they suffer less from the virgin-mother syndrome but nonetheless frequently avoid sex with their spouses after childbirth, my data showing an abrupt 46 percent drop-off rate, as compared with 64 percent for Catholics and 40 percent for Protestants. Most of my male respondents, whether gentile or Jew, were offended or felt uneasy when confronted with this wife-becomes-mother thesis, and some hastily tried to explain their greatly reduced marital intercourse with a wide variety of excuses, some of which are given below:

"Well, to tell you the truth, she wasn't too good after the kid was born. Like she was too loose down there, and there was no friction anymore. I mean it was like screwing a glove. So all of this stuff about her being my own mother is a lotta weirdo crap."

"There's no question we intercoursed a lot less after my kid was born, but that wasn't exactly my fault you know, Rosie wanted it that way. All she could think about was that baby. I was out of it, and I really couldn't touch her without some big scene. So naturally I went somewhere else."

"Come to think about it, I did look at her in a different way. She sort of looked like a madonna when she was holding the baby, especially when she was feeding him. She had this marvelous gentle expression in her face. And I guess it made me think of her—well, not like my own mother, but like a real madonna."

"You sound like this psych professor who was always looking for some weird explanation for anything that came up. Well, as far as I'm concerned, when your wife gets loose from having kids, which you have to expect, then you naturally lose interest. You don't need an Oedipus complex to explain that. Anyway, there's really no resemblance between my wife and my mother—except that they both make good chicken soup."

"I don't know why we quit having sex after the kids were born. I loved her even more, and she was just as tight down there, so that wouldn't be the reason. And it really hurt her—I mean she really wanted me. Yet the harder I tried, the worse it got. So after a while we sort of declared a truce. Then all of a sudden, she'd fly off the handle for no reason, at least none that I could see, 'cause that's the way women are. She'd even get sore when I'd call her 'Mommy' and stuff like that."

"Well, after the kids were born, I figured she didn't need me as much as before, which was natural. After all, she had them to love as well as me. So we didn't have as much sex as before, even though Debby would get horny now and then—but then I'd be too tired, you know. And that's because I was spending more time at my plant, making more loot for my family. But then Debby would gripe 'cause she figured I was balling one of my models, which wasn't always true. But what're you going to tell a wife who won't believe anything?"

"Maybe you're right about this wife-mother idea. Like when I started calling Ellen 'Mommy' after the baby was born, she started calling me 'Daddy,' and it was sort of cute. And a lot of couples do that. Then all of a sudden one day, she got sort of gripey and told me not to call her 'Mommy' anymore. 'But you are a mommy,' I said, sort of grinning. 'That's true,' she said, 'but I'm not your mommy—and I don't want to be treated like her.' So I stopped calling her that, sort of assuming she just didn't like to be compared to my mother, whom she hated—but I never once thought about it in a sexual way. But I guess that could explain why I didn't want her as much as before. After all, she did seem to be more like a mommy than a wife."

The virgin-mother complex has ramifications beyond the sexual relations between husband and wife. Attitudes toward stepchildren, for example, can be strongly affected by prior conditioning. Men are less accepting of a stepchild than women are, perhaps because many men are more affected by any reminders of their wives' prior sexual experience. Consciously or unconsciously, they want virgin wives. In this respect, Jewish men are more insistent than Protestants (55 to 40 percent); but neither compare with the high percentage of Catholics (70 percent) who insist that their brides be virgins. (My fellow Mexicans, most of whom are Catholics, are literally obsessive in their insistence on having virginal brides. Some indeed will refuse to marry fiancées whom they themselves have seduced, the reasoning being, "If you did it for me, you've done it for someone else.")

Needless to say, their high hopes are extremely quixotic if one takes into account the actual statistical evidence of premarital intercourse by women of all religious persuasions. On the other hand, as John Steinbeck whimsically suggested in one of his short stories, there are virgins "by intention" as well as virgins in fact, so that virginity is merely a state of mind. One can easily imagine a woman earnestly telling a new lover, "I'm *your* virgin now, and that's all that matters, honey."

## ORAL SEX WITH FEMALES

As one might expect, oral eroticism also varies according to socioeconomic class and ethnic origin. Adult male Jews, for example, are more active participants in various types of oral sex than are male WASPs; but this may be attributed to economic status rather than ethnic propensity. Whatever reasons one may choose to explain these class and ethnic variations, my composite data cast a revealing light on several specific areas. (In the table that follows, one may for convenience parallel "lower" with grade-school education, "middle" with high-school education and "upper" with college education.)

| Technique | Social Class | Age 18–30 | Age 31–50 | Age 50 + |
|-----------|--------------|-----------|-----------|----------|
| French Kiss | Upper | 75% | 65% | 40% |
| | Middle | 58 | 45 | 30 |
| | Lower | 40 | 30 | 20 |
| Fondle Breast | Upper | 95 | 80 | 50 |
| | Middle | 90 | 75 | 40 |
| | Lower | 80 | 70 | 30 |
| Kiss Breast | Upper | 82 | 70 | 40 |
| | Middle | 52 | 40 | 25 |
| | Lower | 30 | 20 | 10 |
| Touch Genitalia | Upper | 90 | 80 | 40 |
| | Middle | 80 | 70 | 35 |
| | Lower | 72 | 60 | 25 |
| Kiss Genitalia | Upper | 30 | 40 | 15 |
| | Middle | 10 | 15 | 8 |
| | Lower | 8 | 5 | 3 |

Within the categories shown in the foregoing table, the data suggest that college-educated Catholic and Jewish males are more oral than WASPs in the same class; and high-school-educated Jews are more oral than Catholics or WASPs. But among males with only a grade-school education, there is no distinction between Jews and gentiles in their general disdain for oral sex, particularly with respect to cunnilingus.

Most mouth-genital contacts are experienced by married couples, but some men have such contacts only with prostitutes. However, since most prostitutes come from lower socioeconomic groups, very few of them willingly engage in oral activities. Some dislike even French kissing. Even among those who submit to cunnilingus or perform fellatio for paying customers, very few would engage in such activity with their boyfriends. As Kinsey put it, "In her private life, even the prostitute does not depart from the mores of her social level, although she may do anything for pay." Adult males, whether Jew or gentile, tend to follow the same societal pattern of behavior, as evidenced by the following comments in our survey:

"Like I know some chicks go for French kissing and that kinda stuff. But that's kinda sloppy to me, with all that spit causing germs. So the way I figure it, screwing is screwing, and who needs all that other crap. On the other hand, if you gotta suck her tongue to get in her pants, then you go along with it."

"There's some girls that like their nipples kissed and played with. But to tell you the truth, I feel like a goddamned baby sucking a tit. I mean it really turns me off when some gal asks me to do that."

"Quite frankly, the foreplay is just as exciting for me as it is for my wife. I love to feel her nipples harden between my lips and to feel her body beginning to squirm. As for going down on her, I really hesitated at first—but when I realized how excited she got, I got turned on myself. But I can't always do it."

"Listen, man, you've gotta be some kinda queer to go down on a dame. There was this one time that I tried it, when I was in France after the invasion, and I was too drunk, too damned drunk, to know what I was doing. But I got so disgusted doing it, I vomited all over my uniform and couldn't touch no food for almost a week."

"As a lifelong civil libertarian, I have always believed in equal play for male and female. If she pleasures me, I pleasure her."

"According to the Talmud, I have an obligation to take care of my wife's sexual needs at least once a week. That's because I'm a scholar and thus have a lesser quantitative obligation than a plumber or a garbage collector. But since the Talmud says nothing explicit about oral sex, I've given that good book a very liberal interpretation."

"You've gotta be pretty damn queer to go down on someone, especially your own wife. Mine would call me a pervert if I ever tried to."

"Listen, man, all the oral satisfaction I need is a good cigar."

There are, of course, certain types of quasi-erotic oral activities that require no contact with a female, and cigar smoking is one of them. Indeed, some psychologists regard the cigar as a phallic symbol, which may mean that the act of mouthing one is akin to fellatio. In any event, the greatest percentage of cigar smokers (80 percent) are upper- and middle-class males, about evenly divided between gentiles and Jews.* And for some peculiar reason (perhaps narcissism), the entertainment industry has a higher percentage of cigar smokers than any other industry. This is particularly true of Hollywood film producers and directors, most of whom regularly and very ostentatiously lick and mouth their long Havana *perfectos* with great satisfaction. Indeed, one such film-maker fondly refers to his cigar as "my Cuban clit." All of which may confound the aforementioned psychologists who opt for a phallic symbolism.

## RESPONSE TO FELLATIO
## BY FEMALE PARTNER

Although there is a pervasive inequality between men and women in almost every aspect of sexual behavior, the double standard is especially apparent when one considers oral sex. There is a high percentage of males willing to accept fellatio by a female partner, but a much lower percentage willing to perform cunnilingus. Strangely enough (or perhaps not strange at all, but actually predictable), most of my respondents expressed no sense of unfairness in this regard. In fact, 70 percent of them felt that they were accommodating a basic female desire when they permitted themselves to be loved in this manner.

"I don't particularly care for it—but it turns her on, so I let her."

"Well, I let my girl go down on me once in a while. But if my wife ever tried to do it, I'd knock the crap out of her. I really would."

"Like any other guy, I kinda like it when some gal does it to me. But I'd never let my girl friend do it—not in a million years."

"I know it's unfair not to reciprocate when she does it to me. And I've tried a couple of times. But it really turned me off. I almost got sick. So she's never asked me to try again. But I guess it's still not fair."

"In our marriage, everything is *quid quo pro*. Sometimes it's more of her quid than my quo, but I always try to do my share. And, frankly, I like all of it."

Here again, the data reflect a socioeconomic bias. For example, college-educated males usually accept fellatio as a part of their normal sexual experience; whereas high-school-educated males

*However, one should bear in mind the high cost of cigars, which would inevitably diminish the number of cigar smokers in the working class.

are less apt to accept it, and males with lesser education regard it as something bordering on perversion or, indeed, as actual perversion. Since there is a higher percentage of Jewish males in the upper educational strata, one might expect a statistical tilt in their direction; but within each of these educational categories, there is no discernible difference between gentiles and Jews.

## CLITORAL OR VAGINAL STIMULATION IN FOREPLAY

In view of the continuing controversy over the relative merits of clitoral or vaginal orgasms, most of which has been prompted by the Women's Liberation Movement, one should note that adult Jewish males have a marked preference for clitoral stimulation. Since this is also true of upper-class males, we must once again speculate on the comparative influence of socioeconomic and ethnocultural factors. In so doing, we might profitably consider the following statistical data culled from interviews during the past five years. One should bear in mind, of course, the possibility of shifts in attitudes from time to time, particularly in an era of fast-changing mores. Here, then, are some of the findings.

About 55 percent of the Jewish respondents regularly practice clitoral rather than vaginal stimulation, as compared with 45 percent of the Catholics and 40 percent of the Protestants. But within specific socioeconomic levels, the differences are so minimal as to be statistically insignificant. Moreover, less than 10 percent of any ethnic group attempt to induce orgasm through this particular type of foreplay, no doubt assuming that orgasms can be induced solely through actual intercourse—a very macho assumption that has been thoroughly discredited by Masters and Johnson, Dr. Helen Singer Kaplan and, more recently, Shere Hite. Yet, in spite of recent campaigns promoting clitoral orgasms as the *sine qua non* of feminine sexuality, most men doggedly adhere to traditional patterns of foreplay, turning deaf ears to wifely hints or flat-out requests, and often taking manly refuge in outright sarcasm:

"Listen, any woman that can't get ready with just a little necking—and maybe a little finger lovin'—is probably a cold fish."

"There's a lotta women who get warmed up with just a couple of French kisses and a body rub. They don't need all this clit nonsense my wife's been talking about. That's for dames who're frigid."

"There's no question that women need more time to get aroused, and I've really tried to accommodate my woman. But sometimes I keep trying and trying, til my damned middle finger starts to cramp, and then I'm liable to lose my own erection waiting for her to come. So we both end up saying, 'Relax, relax—you're trying too hard!' But how can you in the middle of all that?"

"The worst part of this clitoral thing is trying to time yourself, so that you can come together. Like I'm ready to go from the minute she touches me. But she's got a different rhythm, and it's a lot slower than mine. And when she senses my impatience and a sudden fear of losing my excitement, she naturally gets panicky and starts trying too hard and probably starts to fake it. So the whole damn thing can be a washout. I wish to hell the good Lord had given us sex organs with the same rhythm."

"It isn't enough that you know about the female anatomy. I'm a doctor and I can draw you a perfect cross section of the genital nerve system. But I still can't please my wife or my nurse, no matter how hard I try. My wife says my fingers feel like rubber sausages, and my nurse doesn't say anything."

Some of my respondents' comments suggest deep layers of suppressed hostility, with sex serving as an instrument of aggression or defense for either party. Until fairly recently much of this sexual antagonism has been disguised as not-so-subtle humor by women-hating nightclub comedians or writers of screen scenarios or plays, their efforts often abetted by the female victims themselves. And with the recent female counterattack, angrily led by members of Women's Liberation groups, the conflict has become more heated but less illuminating. When, for example, the somewhat polemical Hite Report was published, certain male writers instantly reacted with sarcasm. Note, for example, the remarks of Gerald Nachman in the New York *Daily News*:

*First off, female sexuality is in real trouble, at least in America. I'm told by my sources that things are not much better in Europe, but Italy and Sweden are doing pretty well (nice work, fellas!).*

*Indeed, according to the late reports just in, female-male sexuality was off 27 points as of yesterday at 3:00 P.M., when trading closed, and falling rapidly.*

*It's expected to pick up again slightly around Christmastime, then fade quickly right after the holiday rush.*

*According to the "Hite Report," men are not pleasing women in certain ways that I'd rather not mention right now, when the girls are present. Suffice it to say that whatever men are doing, it's all wrong and—well, the women are beginning to catch on.*

*Men (if I may digress for just a moment) are starting to wonder how to respond to females who have just read the latest sex survey. Many women, it seems, are turning on to sex studies for kicks, in place of men; they find statistics more stimulating and responsive to their needs.*

*The crux of the "Hite Report" is that males and females are incompatible, which is not a healthy sign. Luckily, we all found this out before it's too late, but now the question before us is: What do we plan to do about it? And where?*

## THE USE OF STREET LANGUAGE_____

Although Herodotus made no specific reference to masculine sexual slang in his chronicles of ancient Greece, one can be sure that the warriors of Sparta and Athens were as bawdy in their speech as the meanest top sergeant in the U.S. Army. Tough, sex-oriented talk has always played a dominant role in the daily conversations of military camps, athletic locker rooms, men's bars and any other exclusively male arena. And, of course, the genital organs of both men and women have been the basic elements of this oral graffiti. Women, with the possible exception of prostitutes and neighborhood chippies, were generally considered too delicate for such language. But in recent years we have witnessed a radical change in the linguistic mores of both sexes, with many women adopting the full range of male slang. Indeed, for some couples, the use of "dirty words" has become an aphrodisiac, particularly the short Anglo-Saxon equivalents of penis and vagina.

Though most ethnic groups have their own piquant synonyms for these genital organs, blacks and Jews have been uniquely creative in this respect. How can one improve on the Yiddish slang words for penis (*shlong*) or limp penis (*schmuck*)?* And what could be more suggestive than the black English word for penis, "Johnson," which may refer to the oft-repeated rumor that Lyndon Johnson once laid his penis on a table be-

*We're informed that *shlong* generally means "snake," and that *schmuck* literally means "jewel."

fore several reporters to prove that it was large enough to lay on a table. In a more onomatopoeic vein is the word "cooz," which blacks rhyme with the word booze when they airily insist that their women want only cooz and booze. But even supposedly liberated males have some reservations about the use of bawdy language in the bedroom.

"I'll have to admit that I sometimes say cunt or prick when I'm having sex with someone—but I'd never let my wife use that kinda language."

"Those kind of words seem to excite a gal, and I get pretty excited myself when I say them. But afterwards I sort of feel funny about saying them—like it wasn't quite right."

"Women get a big charge from that kind of talk. It makes them feel like whores. And when they start yelling those words, they sound like whores, which can really turn you on."

"There's no reason why women shouldn't be as vulgar as men— and nowadays they generally are."

"I used to lay this preacher's daughter, and she was the one who asked me to use all those dirty words. She'd been taught a little Yiddish by some other guy in the Tau Eps fraternity, so she'd always start hollering, 'Give me that big shlong, baby!'—and that would really give me a charge, man."

"I've been asked to use those four-letter words by two different women, but I somehow can't get myself to say them—at least not to a woman I really like."

## REACTION TO PORNO FILMS AND LITERATURE

Although men are far more addicted to pornographic films and literature than women are, less than 10 percent of American males regularly attend porno movie houses or read hardcore pornography, such as *Screw* magazine. Thus, with male porn fans outnumbering female fans by 15 or 20 to 1, we can assume that less than 1 percent of the female population indulges in this particular aspect of erotic behavior. This does not necessarily mean that women are less interested in the sadomasochism that is so pervasive in such films or magazines; it may simply mean that societal strictures are still so severe as to totally discourage women from attending so-called adult movie theatres or from buying porno magazines at newsstands.

Moreover, many possibly interested women may be deterred by the implicit or explicit disapproval of husbands or male companions, as one may gather from the following comments from some of my male respondents:

"I saw a porno film in Frisco with some other Teamster buddies; but, frankly, they're not for me. All that crude sex really depressed me, though Greg and Ernie laughed like goddamned hyenas. So I guess it's a taste you've got to develop, which I probably won't."

"There are some people who get squeamish about a little sado-masochism, but I think these films are just a put-on, a real satire on the leather freaks. And all that violence isn't half as bad as what you see on the six o'clock news."

"About two years ago I took this chick to a porno movie on La Cienega, naïvely assuming that she'd get turned on. But she made us leave the damned show less than ten minutes after it started, and I couldn't get her near my pad after that. Like I'd really figured her as a cool chick, but she must have taken me for a dirty old man. So you never know."

"Just after I got married, me and my cousin Joey went to a porno movie downtown, and suddenly I saw this woman who looked exactly like my wife sitting near the other exit. Jeez, that really got me—I mean my own wife in a place like that! Shit, man, that's enough to freak you out. But when I checked her out—and I mean right away—I saw it was somebody else. Probably some whore lookin' to score with one of those bald-headed guys jerking himself off in the back row."

Curiously enough, WASP porno fans outnumber Jews and Catholics by nearly 2 to 1, which may reflect a more furtive, less open attitude toward sex in general. Many of my Jewish interviewees who frankly and very casually discussed all aspects of their sexual behavior almost unanimously scoffed at the idea of seeing porno films on a more-than-once basis. "That's for people who can't make it with other people," one of them said. "Now, who would want to sit in the dark wanging his schlong when he can get a woman to do it for him? That's the kind of guy who likes to look at someone else doing what he'd like to do himself or have done to him. Usually some timid church-going type who's too uptight to do anything except jerk off." When I later observed scores of men and very few women entering and leaving two porno movie theatres on Forty-second Street, I was inclined to agree with his hunch.

# SEX CONTACT WITH ANIMALS_____

Although Alfred Kinsey reported a surprisingly high incidence of sexual contacts with animals in his study of American males, there was an almost total absence of such activity admitted to by the men I interviewed. This is probably due to the fact that this survey was concentrated in urban areas; most of the sodomy cases reported by Kinsey occurred in rural areas, where men and boys are in constant contact with farm animals.

# MALE IGNORANCE OF FEMALE NEEDS_____

Time and again my interviews revealed that most men are unaware of their mates' real sexual responses. When a man has a sexual problem, his wife or female companion probably knows about it, but the man rarely recognizes his partner's problems. This was borne out by a study of 100 white, middle-class Christian couples conducted by the University of Pittsburgh's Department of Psychiatry and published in the *New England Journal of Medicine*.

One-third of the women surveyed said that they had difficulty maintaining excitement in intercourse, but only one husband in seven thought his wife had this problem.

Although almost half the women and one-third of the men reported physical or psychological problems with sex, 83 men and 83 women rated their marriages as happy. Ninety percent said that they would marry the same person if they had their lives to live over.

The study concluded that the couples "still feel very positive about their sexual relations and their marriages."

The researchers found that difficulty in becoming aroused was the most important factor in a woman's sexual dissatisfaction, more important than difficulty or inability to reach orgasm.

Nearly half the women said that they had difficulty getting aroused, and 46 of those questioned had difficulty reaching an orgasm. The women also said that they could not relax during sex and complained of too little foreplay and too little tenderness after intercourse.

The most frequent problem among the men, listed by 36 of them, was premature ejaculation. Sixteen percent said they had difficulty getting an erection or difficulty maintaining one.

The average age of the women surveyed was 35, that of the men, 37.

The researchers cautioned that the 100 couples should not be considered typical because they were "all well-educated, relatively comfortable couples who believe that their marriages are working."

It is also acknowledged that there was a risk in asking people to rate their own marriages.

The study identified two types of sex problems: dysfunctions, such as erectile and ejaculatory problems in the male and arousal and orgasmic problems in the females; and difficulties, such as inability to relax, inconvenience, disinterest, too little foreplay and too little tenderness.

The study said that although wives might suffer their sexual dysfunctions in silence, sexual difficulties were apt to color the couple's relations.

"Among all the possible kinds of sexual problems, it is clearly the wives' sexual 'difficulties' that were the least well tolerated," the study indicated, going on to conclude:

*Indeed, they seem to have a ripple effect on all sexual relations. Although it was once thought it was the man who wrote, produced and performed the sexual scenario, with the wife acting the role of "extra," at least within this better educated, more affluent population, the wife emerged as the major influence on the course of the drama.*

*If the women was unable to relax, felt "turned-off" or was approached at the wrong time, all sexual relations suffered as a result.*

But a study of young, college-age couples indicates that the man sets the stage for sexual relations—that despite the apparent breakdown of the double standard, the male is expected to make the first move.

In a two-year study of 200 couples in the Boston area, directed by UCLA Professor Letitia Anne Peplau and two other social psychologists—Professor Zick Rubin of Brandeis University and Professor Charles T. Hill of the University of Washington—it was found that 95 percent of the women waited for the men to make sexual overtures, fearing that the male ego would be threatened if they acted first.

"There are no easy rules to explain why people do what they do," Professor Peplau wrote in *The Journal of Social Issues*, "but I think women fear that to violate standards of traditional behavior could be to invite misunderstanding. If the woman should suddenly become the initiator of sex, some men would feel threatened."

She added: "Sexual role-playing provides a familiar, understandable set of guidelines for male-female interactions."

The study also found that when a couple began having sex—or whether they abstained—had no effect on the durability of their relationship. Of the couples in the study, 41 percent had sex within a month of meeting, 41 percent began having sex after a month and 18 percent abstained. But over the two-year period, 46 percent of each group broke up, 34 percent were still dating and 20 percent got married.

"We found no evidence that early sex necessarily short-circuits the development of lasting commitments or that sexual abstinence or moderation increases or decreases the development of a lasting relationship," Professor Peplau concluded.

# 4
# Interethnic Sex

When *Portnoy's Complaint* was first published several years ago, many Jews felt that Philip Roth had committed an act of betrayal against his own people, that he had drawn a vicious caricature of the already much maligned Jewish mother and that he had grossly exaggerated the Jewish males' so-called shiksa complex. It is with this latter phenomenon that we are presently concerned, and Roth's controversial novel offers a convenient point of departure.

As one may recall, young Portnoy did indeed have an erotic obsession about gentile girls with blue eyes and blonde hair, and his fantasies about them were absolutely hilarious. But they were gross exaggerations and were obviously intended to be. Still, there was a kernel of truth in Roth's wild inventions, as there must be in any successful satire, and he was probably delving into his own humorously remembered teenage notions about the mythic charms of shiksas.

Although "shiksaphilia" may affect only a small percentage of Jewish males, mostly in their late teens and early twenties, there are some adults who suffer from this affliction until late in life. I have in mind a forty-five-year-old psychoanalyst whom I met in an enclave of analysts spending their obligatory August-away-from Manhattan on the sandy stretch of East Hampton. As I was chatting with Dr. X on the terrace of his beachside cottage, he suddenly looked away from me and stared at a slender blonde walking near the water, her beautifully tanned body glistening in the late afternoon sunlight.

"There's another shiksa," he said, more to himself than to me. "The kind you dream about."

Then he turned and smiled rather sheepishly, his voice still muted to a near whisper. "I've always had this obsession with slender, blue-eyed blondes—ever since my high-school days. They remind me of this shiksa cheerleader I tried to date, and never could. There were other shiksas I could have screwed—really easy lays—but not the one I wanted. Every time I started to ask her, she'd make me feel awkward and Jewish, so I finally quit trying."

"But you've probably had others," I said, sensing that he was confiding in me only because I was a stranger.

"Well, I've had seven or eight shiksas in the past few years—maybe more—but not the kind I really want. I mean like that girl who just walked past us."

"Have you tried?" I asked.

"Wouldn't do any good," he said. "I'd get all tied up in knots, afraid she might think I'm not her type."

Apparently, his obsession was common gossip within his crowd, because the following night, as I was talking to his wife and two other women at a beach party, his wife suddenly interrupted the conversation with a joking comment about her husband: "There's Sam again, staring at that blonde shiksa in the no-back dress. I wish to hell he'd screw one of them and get this damn fantasy off his mind."

"Why doesn't he?" asked one of her friends.

"Because he's afraid he'll get turned down," the wife answered. "And that would be too much for his frail ego. He's got about the worst shiksa complex I've ever heard of, and he's a fucking analyst, for godsake!"

As was stated in an earlier chapter, about 25 percent of the Jewish male respondents recalled having experienced some degree of shiksaphilia, the severity of the symptoms often disappearing upon actual contact with the supposedly unavailable gentile female. As one man ruefully observed, "When I found out they were just as kvetchy as my Jewish girl friends and not half as much fun to joke with, I got over my fixation." As previously noted, many Chicanos and Puerto Ricans are also obsessed with light-skinned, blonde gringas because they are supposedly more amenable to sex than their own virginity-obsessed women.

There were several comments expressing interethnic sexual obsessions, while others reflected a continuing ambivalence and self-reproach:

"As I was finishing law school, I got this screwy notion that I needed a nice little WASP from Wellesley or Vassar to help me make it career-wise. So I tried out a few—even shacked up with one for five months—and finally got hitched to a High Episcopalian from Boston, who got high at our wedding and never seemed to get sober again. So we finally got divorced, and I got myself a nice Italian girl, who may not be a blonde and slender but who sure as hell isn't an alcoholic."

"Why the hell should I kid you? I *do* have a letch for shiksas, especially if they're blonde and sort of classy-looking. But I'd never marry one, 'cause you never know when they might get sore at you and start calling you a dirty Jew or something worse. So they're okay for one-nighters or maybe an affair, if you can afford that sort of thing. But not for something permanent. It's better to stick with your own kind for the long haul."

"Look, I'm married to a Catholic, and I would never think of her as a shiksa, which is really an insulting term. So, as far as I'm concerned, this ethnic crap is for the birds. I mean it's not relevant."

"When I met Fran I never gave her religion a second thought. She was just a woman to me, a very tender and lovely woman. I really didn't know what she was until her mother started making arrangements for a Catholic wedding, and Fran told her to cool it. Then my mother started talking about a Jewish ceremony. So we finally got married near Walden Pond, with only poetry and music and no preacher of any kind."

"To tell you the truth, I'm still hung up on gringas, and all my secretaries have been gringas. They give an office a little class, if you know what I mean, especially when they don't have an accent. But when it comes to sex, they look cold as hell to me. For that, you've got to have someone warm and *muy latina*."

"When I was young and more foolish than I am now, the little shiksas looked pretty good to me. But you soon realize that their appeal is all part of that propaganda you get in magazine ads and TV commercials where you get nothing but straight-nose blondes with no tits. And let me tell you something else: Most of your gentiles don't look that way either."

"The way I see it, all women come with the same basic equipment, and the color of their eyes and the shape of their nose don't make a bit of difference. So I really can't understand all this fuss about shiksas. But I've got to admit that I've got an awful letch for Oriental women, especially Eurasians. That's the only reason I hated to leave Saigon."

"I've had my share of gentiles, and I don't find them much different from Jewish women. But, quite frankly, I think all women are pretty expendable."

"A couple of years ago I met this Catholic chick who kept telling me to call her a shiksa while we were screwing. She thought it meant 'whore' and it really turned her on."

"Some day, people won't think about how other people look or what their race or religion is—but I sure hope they don't eliminate gender."

## WHAT THE SHIKSAS THINK _____

Having obtained a comparatively fair sample of what Jewish men think about gentile women, I thought it might be instructive to know how gentile females feel about the Jewish men they have known on a sexual basis. It should be noted that on a rating scale of "excellent," "good," "fair," or "inferior," at least 60 percent of gentile respondents rated their Jewish lovers and husbands as "excellent" or "good."

On the other hand, only 45 percent of the Jewish female respondents placed their Jewish men in those two favorable categories. When informed of this statistical disparity, a New York psychiatric social worker expressed no surprise whatever. "You've got to bear in mind," she said, "that your shiksa interviewees already had a favorable predisposition toward Jewish men when they first went to bed with them. And like many of us, they had heard that Jews are decent husbands and good lovers, even though many of them are goddamned princes. So they're in a plus mood to begin with. But because of much more exposure, Jewish women have fewer illusions about their own men. Even so, I'm still surprised that your data shows that forty-five percent of them rate their Jewish husbands and lovers as excellent or good. I'll bet anything that there are much fewer gentile women who rate their men that high. I doubt that more than twenty-five to thirty-five percent would give that favorable a rating. And, if you believe the Hite Report, that might be as low as ten or fifteen percent."

Whether or not these percentages accurately reflect feminine sentiments in all segments of the population, the following spontaneous comments may give us more specific insights than one might expect from any amount of statistical data:

"I know you shouldn't generalize about Jewish men or anyone else, especially if you're a Catholic like me, but I frankly think they make the best husbands. Mine sure is, even when he's bad."

"For a while I thought Sam was merely using me, that I was just another shiksa. But when he found out how much I really loved him, in spite of his cynicism he sort of softened and let himself become lovable."

"I'm not sure I can really trust them. They're so damned moody and unpredictable. But they always seem to get around me, mostly by making me laugh. And they're awfully tender in bed, at least the ones I've known."

"Of course, no one wants to be called a shiksa, but Ron keeps telling me that it's only a term of endearment. Which I think is a lot of bull, but he's awfully sweet when he says it. Anyway, he's about the only man I know who's willing to have sex my way."

"If his damn mother would stay away from us, Stan and I would have no problems. But when she's around he acts like a spoiled brat. He's even lousy in bed when that kvetch stays overnight. He's actually afraid she'll hear us humping."

"None of my gentile girl friends at school thought I was serious about Aaron. They just assumed I was temporarily overwhelmed by all that poetry he used to spout. Well, we've been married twenty years and I have four teenagers, and he still recites poetry in bed."

## GENTILE MEN AND JEWISH WOMEN_____

Although a considerable number of Jewish women have had sexual relations with non-Jewish men (perhaps as many as 35 percent), they are seldom accused of having a "goy complex." A few may be called boy crazy but almost never "goy crazy." If, indeed, any significant portion of them do have erotic obsessions about gentile males, they somehow manage to keep it to themselves, without bruiting it about and creating the kind of hullabaloo which has characterized the so-called shiksa complex. Perhaps one reason for this curious disparity is that there are few, if any, parental strictures against Jewish males having sex with gentiles, whereas Jewish females are constantly admonished to preserve their chastity for someone within their own group.

Notwithstanding such parental admonitions, thousands of Jewish women have had gentile lovers and have occasionally married them. And judging from the data gathered in this survey, they have achieved an extremely favorable rating from their cross-ethnic lovers. About 70 percent of our non-Jewish male respondents rate them as "excellent" or "good," as compared with a 45 percent favorable rating among men from their own cultural background. Here, again, one may argue that the aforementioned gentiles were already favorably disposed to

Jewish women (for any number of reasons) and were thus likely to reinforce their prior attitudes. Be that as it may, their informal comments add a bit of flesh to the skeletal statistics:

"As a middle-class WASP from the Midwest, I was really rattled by the first Jewish girl I ever dated. She was so goddamned frank and open about sex—I mean the way she used words that only men are supposed to use—well, that sort of caught me off guard. And even when I realized that she wasn't about to go all the way in spite of our hot necking sessions, I still hung in there. 'Cause, quite frankly, I liked the way she talked about sex—it was almost like getting laid. And all the others, at least the ones I've met, are pretty much the same. As for actual screwing, I get most of that from one of those quiet Catholic girls, who doesn't talk much but screws like a mink. And once in a while I score with a Jewish woman who's married and bored and wants only sex—no romance, just sex."

"My first affair with a Jewish girl was back in college. We worked on the campus newspaper together and we were always joking about sex and occasionally telling each other the latest dirty jokes, of which she knew a lot more than I did. Then one night, out at the printing plant, we suddenly started necking—without any prelude. It just happened. Well, a few days after that, she came up to my room and we went all the way. And that's when I found out she was a virgin—this sexy-talking little thing was still a virgin, at least until that particular afternoon. But once she lost her cherry, there was no stopping her, and she was fabulous. I still think about Sharon now and then, and often wish we'd gotten married."

"For all-around relationship, I'll take a Jewish woman any day. They may bitch now and then—but all women do."

"Compared to some of the girls I grew up with back in Iowa, Jewish women are a lot more interesting and even sexier—when they finally decide to do it. But I'm sometimes put off when they start joking about sex—like when some gal starts calling your pecker funny names like 'shmuck' or 'shlong' or something else."

"They have bigger breasts and sexier eyes—but I don't like it when they have a nose bob. It throws their face out of proportion."

"Now that I've had three Jewish girl friends and lived with one for three months, this Catholic I'm dating seems awfully shy and uptight."

"I think Jewish women come on too strong, like they want to take charge of everything. This one chick was so goddamned bossy, she even wanted to tell me how to screw her. Like 'touch me there—no, not there, up a little higher and don't stop til I tell you.' And all that sorta crap. Like I'm some kinda mechanic who's just there to service her private parts."

"When I first met Mitzi, I thought she was really turned on by me. But I soon found out she was nothing but a tease. All talk and no action."

"There's nothing like tender and funny love-making, and that's what you're apt to get with a Jewish woman."

"Some day I'd like to meet one who doesn't analyze sex to a complete vacuum. I've lost more hard-ons listening to some dame trying to figure out why she's in bed with you."

"I've always liked them because they like to experiment with all kinds of different positions that I've never tried before. But sixty-nine is not for me."

"Frankly, I can't stand women who want a damn explanation for everything, especially when you're already in the sack."

That last comment reminds us of E. B. White's remark in his essay "Is Sex Necessary?" "By and large," he said, "love is easier to experience before it has been explained—easier and cleaner."

## INTERRACIAL SEX

### Sex With Blacks

Interracial sex has been practiced for thousands of years and was probably initiated by soldiers of the first army that ever conquered another tribe. Usually, such copulation has been forced upon the females of the oppressed group by well-armed male oppressors, with little thought or concern given to the children born. Some countries—Mexico, for example—are almost completely populated by the mestizo offspring of former conquerors. And in the United States, millions of black men and women are descendents of white men who either raped or seduced their female slaves or employees. Interestingly enough, the dark-skinned males of the oppressed group seldom had sexual relations with the lighter-skinned females of the dominant group; and if they did, their relations were extremely furtive and indeed dangerous, for the taboo against "race mixing" of that kind was (and generally still is) obsessively mandated.

Such taboos are still very much in force, but they have been increasingly violated in recent years, particularly within certain middle- and upper-class groups. For example, there has been a marked increase in the number of black men dating and/or marrying white women, but there have been far fewer white men having open sexual relations with black women, that inverse ratio probably approximately 1 to 20. Among the Chicanos in this country, that ratio is close to parity, with just as many Chicanas dating Anglo men as Chicanos dating Anglo women; but until fairly recently, most well-educated Chicanos tended to marry Anglo women.

Needless to say, many of the black-white sexual unions occurred as a direct result of the Civil Rights Movement, which brought together thousands of white and black militants, their political fervor often (and perhaps inevitably) spilling over into a different level of emotion. But, even within this supposedly egalitarian ambiance, there were many more black men than black women crossing the racial barrier sexually. Some psychologists explain this disparity as just another example of "a more basic liberality" or "more experimental attitudes about sex" among women. Some observers feel that white females were heavily pressured by black men to prove their radical liberalism by going to bed with them, on the grounds that to resist would be proof of suspect and phony idealism. Still others insist that such women were magnetized by the Black Power mystique and thoroughly enjoyed the sexual imperative, much to the silent and impotent rage of their white male partisans.

Since traditionally liberal Jews far outnumbered any other white group in their support of the Civil Rights Movement, Jewish female liaisons with black men have been proportionately more numerous than similar relations involving gentile women. On a per capita basis, the ratio could be as high as 4 to 3, although no specific data is available. Within the gentile group, WASP females were more likely to have black lovers than Catholic females. But one must bear in mind that only a very small percentage of white women—perhaps less than 5 percent—have admitted to being involved in interracial sex: and most of that 5 percent were women with middle-class backgrounds and some degree of college education. Moreover, many of these sexual involvements have had no connection with political militancy. Indeed, some of them were motivated by nothing more than rebellion against parental control, a transitory period of identity confusion or (if they are closet racists) a neurotic need for self-abasement. Blacks, of course, have been keenly aware of these mixed and negative motives and consequently have warily avoided deep commitments. Small wonder that interracial ventures have led to infinitely complex emotional muddles which, in turn, have stirred deep anger, fear and resentment, unbearably poignant hope and an occasional profound love that has overcome all obstacles. The following excerpts from numerous interviews offer only a hint of the conflicting attitudes of people involved therein:

"When I finally forced myself to face the truth, I realized that all my affairs with black men were really meant to hurt my dad, to get him really pissed off. And yet I tried to convince myself that I really loved Floyd and Willie and Russ, even when they treated me like shit and called me a funky white bitch and sometimes slapped me around. But even knowing this, I'm still doing the same thing and hating myself for deceiving everyone involved."

"Listen, man, I knew she was using me to get back at her folks for whatever they'd done to fuck up her mind. But I was using her, too, so it was even-steven."

"How can you really tell if some chick actually loves you or is just trying to prove she ain't prejudiced? Well, that sort of bothered me at first, but I'm not about to pass up some white sugar just because of that. Love or no love, my pecker makes no distinction."

"I know it's hard for my dad and mom to believe that I really love Wally, that I'm not trying to prove what a big liberal I am. But what really bothers me most is when Wally himself starts joking about us and sometimes implies that I'm just a freak for black sex—whatever that is. I don't know if I can ever convince him that color doesn't mean a damn thing to me."

"Debby and I were going to be married, but we postponed our wedding for a couple of months so we could join the Freedom Marches down south. Then she met this black guy on a picket line and she went off her rocker. She actually chased after that mother, and finally started shacking with him. And when he pushed her off, she found herself another black lover, whom I never knew because I'd split that scene. Then a couple of years later she comes back and expects me to marry her after all. Well, man, I really told her where to head off. Like I'm still a liberal mind you, but no way am I going to play second fiddle to a big-dick *shwartze*—not even to Sammy Davis, who's one of us."

"To tell you the truth, I got myself more sex from the Civil Rights Movement than any dude I know. Those white chicks were civil and right and had all the movement you ever dreamed about. And, let me tell you, those white guys hated our guts but wouldn't dare admit it."

"I've been in love with this marvelous black woman for about ten years; but I know I'll never marry her, that we'll always be seeing each other on the sly. My kids would crucify me if they ever found out about Laura, even though they've been trying to get me married off since a couple of years after my wife died."

"There's no point denying that I've always had a yen for black men, ever since high school. They've always seemed sexier, stronger, and more in control of themselves. But I've only fantasized about them. And sometimes when I'm having sex with Stanley, I imagine he's someone like O.J. Simpson or Sidney Poitier."

"I'm not that way about black men, but I really dig Chicanos. They're darker than me but not too dark."

"As a black woman, I've got every right to hate all these sex-starved honky bitches who come chasing after our men."

"How are you going to compete with these pale-eyed, thin-lipped, blonde bitches who've got our black men acting like goddamned fools?"

"When I found out that my fiancée had once screwed around with a black guy, I called it off. Not that I expected a virgin, but I figured he'd given her the kinda sex I couldn't give her—so why kid myself."

"Max knows that I've been around men. After all, I was a model in the garment industry. But if I ever told him about that colored dentist I met in San Juan, he'd dump me right now."

"I'd rather have a woman my own color, 'cause I really believe that black is beautiful. But I've gotten so screwed up by the standards of this white society that I can't even get an erection with a black woman. Only a goddamned white bitch can make me respond sexually, and I'm not the only dude who's got that problem."

Many Chicanos and Chicanas are faced with similar dilemmas, particularly in Texas and Arizona, but they are much less severe or traumatic. And Anglo women dating or marrying Chicanos are not so apt to be ostracized by relatives and friends than when they form sexual liaisons with black men.

*Sex With Orientals*

During the American occupation of Japan after World War II, thousands of our soldiers were beguiled by the winsome femininity of Japanese women, many of whom subsequently came to the U.S. as "GI brides." Some American men, having been exposed to the quiet, submissive manner of the Oriental women they met, were never thereafter satisfied with the more independent (sometimes demanding) girl friends and wives back home.

Among them was a prominent war correspondent (we'll call Jim Weeks) who fell desperately in love with a delicate beauty he had met in a nightclub where geisha girls served patrons with exquisite attentiveness. "I spent hours and hours with Michi at the club," he later told a friend, "and finally persuaded her to quit her job as a geisha and move in with me. And, believe me, it was heaven. I had never been treated with such devotion. After we'd had sex, she would gently bathe my body with warm cologne-scented towels, and then she'd massage my back until I'd finally doze off into the most peaceful sleep you can possibly imagine. And while I slept, she would prepare a fantastic snack (or a whole meal, depending on the hour), which she would serve me with that quiet delicate grace that only Oriental women have. But aside from the sex and the food, she was a marvelous housekeeper—kept everything absolutely neat and clean. And she never bitched about anything, never begged me . . . the most wonderful woman I'd ever met."

Eventually his tour of duty came to an end, and he was assigned to Los Angeles; but he asked for an extended assignment in Tokyo, which his immediate boss (and close friend) refused. "You've got a lovely wife and three kids at home," he told Weeks, "and they need you." Most reluctantly, Weeks gave up the idea of divorcing his wife of fifteen years to marry Michi, but he never really reconciled himself to his marriage. "American women are such bitches," he told a colleague. "They are always demanding this or that, pushing you night and day, and yacking their head off. And, mind you, Jane is about as good a gal as you can expect in this fucking town—but she's still an American!"

Such high regard for Oriental women has been voiced repeatedly by thousands of men. Among the more appreciative was a Los Angeles trial lawyer who had had an extended affair with a Eurasian who had been reared in Tokyo and Shanghai. She, too, attended his every need, keeping his apartment spotlessly clean, cooking the finest food he had ever eaten and gently bathing his body with warm scented towels after each sexual act. But her quiet, consuming devotion was eventually too much for him. "I began to feel guilty," he told a colleague. "I just couldn't reciprocate her attentiveness, her uncomplaining submissiveness. And I felt I was taking advantage of her. In fact, I kept hoping she would start to bitch at me—the way American women do. But she never did. So I finally met a spoiled bitchy gal from Denver and married her, and no way can I feel guilty about the way I treat her. I guess when you're raised by a mother who bitches a lot, you kind of expect all women to be like her."

It should be noted that men who lavish praise on Oriental women seldom stress the act of sex itself—the specific physical aspects—but generally emphasize the prelude and the aftermath. And when they talk about being bathed with warm towels, one senses a sort of sensuous regression to infancy.

Apparently, Oriental men do not evoke the same sexual mystique as their female counterparts. Very few American women rave about them as lovers. But in recent years they have been raving about Italian men—not necessarily about the suave Marcello Mastroiani or the comically charming Giancarlo Gianinni, but rather the very earthy, swaggering American-ghetto stud as personified by Sylvester Stallone in *Rocky*. The dark brooding eyes, the inarticulate mumble, the well-muscled body and aggressive swagger seem to connote explosive sexuality to millions of females who flock to movies to see Stallone, John Travolta, Al Pacino, Robert de Niro and several less prominent actors of Italian descent. As one can observe from the following comments, their admirers seem to respond in ways that are less than platonic:

"Rocky can have me anytime—with or without foreplay."
"Travolta is the sexiest guy since Rudolph Valentino, whom I never saw except for what my aunt says."

"The way Travolta walks and dances and that Italian way of look-ing at you—now that's what I call sexy, really sexy."

"I like that Mafia sense of danger in Stallone and Pacino, like they could be mean in a way that wouldn't be too bad."

"Anyone who dances the way Travolta dances, well, he's got to be pretty good in bed."

"Rocky was sort of tough and tender at the same time. He'd probably marry you if he got you pregnant."

"Pacino attracts me more than Stallone because he's more intelli-gent and sensitive—and just as tough. Particularly in *The Godfather*."

Some of the negative comments seem to reflect old stereotypes about this particular ethnic group, some of which unfortu-nately have been re-emphasized in the roles portrayed by Pacino, de Niro, Stallone and Travolta:

"I'm not impressed by that vulgar strutting and tough-guy talk. They look sweaty and probably smell of garlic and cheap wine."

"All those tough and supposedly-sexy Italians in *The Godfather* movies were made more glamorous than they actually are. They're still Mafia hoods with mean macho attitudes, and they treat women like dirt."

"Some women may get excited by dumb sexy punks like Travolta in *Saturday Night Fever*, but I'm turned off by his vulgarity."

"Whenever I see men strutting and swaggering like Travolta and Stallone, I get the impression that they're masking a latent homo tendency."

"I once dated a guy like Travolta in *Saturday Night Fever*." He was also a sexy dancer—but not very good in bed. He'd come in less than a minute and didn't give a damn if I was satisfied. As far as he was concerned, Irish girls were for laying and Italian girls for marrying."

"People like 'The Fonz' and Travolta and Rocky—all those Italian guys who wear black jackets and T-shirts and grease in their hair—may look sexy to some women, but they turn me off."

"Italians think you're either a whore or a virgin, with no in-between. And if you stay a virgin, they might marry you."

Although it is hazardous to draw sociological conclusions from movies, the whore-virgin syndrome surfaces repeatedly in films and novels about Italian-Americans. There is a curious paradoxical morality among members of the Mafia, who studi-ously protect and isolate their wives and daughters from the scum and violence of the narcotics and prostitution rackets they operate. At times their women seem as innocent as nuns, while the men consort with whores or will have well-publicized mistresses. But the mistresses know that their gangster lovers will never divorce their wives, and this is also true in Latin America. This may reflect Catholic strictures against divorce, but it is more likely a sociocultural conviction that their wives were once virgins while their mistresses were always whores. Although most of the Mafia is presumed to be Italian, it constitutes only a minute fraction of 1 percent of the Italian-American population, so that the mores of this much-publicized group are statistically insignificant. Nevertheless, the sexual attitudes and behavior of these notorious racketeers seem to reflect the extremely conservative norms of the neighborhoods in which they have been reared, where the whore-virgin complex is a dominant factor.

# 5

# Age as a Factor in Sexual Behavior

*... the onset of regular sexual performance is usually coinciden-tal with the onset of adolescence. Over 95 percent of the adolescent males are regularly active by 15 years of age. Over 99 percent of the adolescent and older males are active throughout the whole period from 16 to 45. In those 30 years, only 1 or 2 percent of the male population is without regular and usually frequent outlet. After 45 there is a gradual but distinct drop in the number of active cases. These generalizations apply to all white males, whether single or married, and whatever their educational level or social background.*

When Alfred Kinsey made that statement in his instantly fa-mous book on sexual behavior, there were more than a few raised eyebrows among his fellow social scientists, some of whom immediately challenged the validity of his investigative techniques. But his statement seems somewhat less astonishing when one realizes that he was referring to the whole range of sexual activity—petting to climax, masturbation, homosexual outlet and so on—and not just actual intercourse. And the last sentence in his above-quoted statement would seem to run counter to the numerous statistical tables that appear elsewhere in his book and which show considerable differences in the sexual activities of males with different backgrounds and dif-ferent levels of education.

Certainly, my data reveal some significant differences between Jews and gentiles, particularly after adolescence. Since we have dealt with teenage sexuality in Chapter 1, we shall now address ourselves to adult behavior and how it is affected by the aging process.

99

## SEXUAL BEHAVIOR AMONG YOUNG ADULTS___

As indicated in previous chapters, young adult Jews (twenty to thirty years of age) apparently are more sexually active than gentiles in the same age bracket. For example, about 75 percent of Jewish males engage in frequent or moderate intercourse— ranging from several times per week to once a week—as compared with 66 percent of the gentile males of equal age. Among females, the comparative ratio is about the same, 68 percent for Jewish women and 58 percent for gentile women. Within the gentile group, Catholics have a slight edge over WASPs.

For adults between the ages of thirty-one to forty, the ratios seem to be about the same, with Jewish males registering 58 percent; gentiles about 54 percent; Jewish females 48 percent; and gentile women slightly more than 40 percent. Once again, within the gentile group the difference between Catholics and WASPs is minimal. One should note that the lower rate of activity for females may simply reflect a certain modest reluctance to talk about sex, or it may also reflect a bit of macho exaggeration by my male respondents.

With respect to this particular age span, the data relate to marital intercourse, but there is a significant amount of adultery by all ethnic groups throughout adulthood. Nonetheless, there is reason to believe that Jewish men and women are slightly more inclined than WASPs are when it comes to "fishing in other waters," as my godfather used to characterize his pecadillos. (Not surprisingly, *pecadillo* means "little sin" in Spanish, although it is a mortal one in Catholic dogma.)


## MIDDLE-AGED SEXUAL BEHAVIOR _____

Needless to say, the sex lives of most human beings become more difficult and confusing with the onset of middle age. Quite suddenly, around the ominous age of forty, the fear of impotency or greatly diminished sexuality looms on the not-so-distant horizon like a darkening cloud, producing endless anxieties that merely compound the problems that provoked the initial anxiety. One lost erection in precoital foreplay is refracted in multiple mirrors facing each other. (The reference to masculine trauma is intentional, since the male loss of virility is usually more apparent to the naked eye.) And yet there is a comforting number of people who somehow manage to overcome this middle-age malaise.

From the ages of forty-one to sixty (particularly during the earlier decade), about 42 percent of Jewish women and 36 percent of gentile women engage in frequent or moderate intercourse. The percentages for men are slightly higher, with 48 percent for Jews and 43 percent for gentiles. Here again we must bear in mind the probable upward-fudging of the male respondents.

## EXTRAMARITAL RELATIONS

It is during this period that a marked change occurs in the adulterous conduct of both men and women. Prior to the age of forty, most philanderers engage in short-lived affairs, many of which are one-night stands with total strangers. But with the onset of middle age, there is a measurable increase in the percentage of extramarital liaisons of a more serious nature, some of which eventually lead to divorce. Indeed, a sizable proportion of these sexual entanglements involve people who have seldom if ever strayed from home, and come as a complete surprise to the aggrieved spouse. As a former lawyer in divorce-prone Los Angeles, I remember only too well the number of clients who simply couldn't believe that their husbands or wives "wanted out" because of some newfound love. Many hoped that "this middle-age madness" would pass, especially under the threat of divorce and the financial squeeze of a community-property split; but, more often than not, such hopes were soon relinquished. As one forty-five-year-old wife sadly observed, "I was assuming that George was just having a fling with this little chippy who could make him feel like a real man again—but I guess it's something more serious. So I'll find myself a young lover . . . which is some laugh when you consider how little I've got to offer."

My data suggest that Jewish men are apt to have a greater number of brief affairs than either Catholics or Protestants, but Jews are less inclined to get involved in the more serious long-term affairs that eventually cause divorces. On the other hand,

Protestants and Catholics are about equally susceptible to serious extramarital involvements; but, because of religious strictures against divorce, Catholic affairs are much more likely to go on and on, until boredom or resignation take their toll.

Whether brief or prolonged, these middle-age ventures into new sexual and emotional terrain produce a wide range of guilt, ambivalence and/or a welcome relief from less than satisfactory marriage. The following are some expressions of these various attitudes:

"I don't mind his fooling around—well, actually I do mind—but why did he have to pick this fake blonde shiksa who can't even type out a bill of lading? So maybe he'll get bored with her dumbness, on which I'm not counting. He's such a damned fool lately, especially since he started losing his hair."

"At his age, you've got to expect a little hanky-panky with the opposing sex. My uncle and my own father played a little. But when it comes to a serious romance, that I won't put up with. Sex is sex and love is love, and you can't mix the two with some floozy off the street."

"The trouble with Fran is her not understanding that I needed something new in my life. Suddenly, I could feel myself getting flat and stale, so that I couldn't even face my fucking desk in the morning. And then I meet someone who by instinct knows that what my needs are—and not just sex, mind you—but this Fran simply can't understand, even though it may be something temporary that I'll get over sometime. I mean a man's got to have some room."

"Okay, I know a little outside nooky will sometimes make a man feel young again, especially when your own screwing has gotten passé. But why is it the wife who's always supposed to understand and take all that crap?"

"You ever get that feeling that life has passed you by? That you've worked your goddamned ass off for thirty years and what for? Well, when I get that awful down feeling, I just hop a plane to Vegas and get myself laid by one of those beautiful hookers in one of the chorus lines. Costs me a bundle, but I'm a new man—at least for a couple of days. And lately I'm going almost every weekend, which I'm having trouble explaining to the old lady. Like I've never had much business out of town."

"My husband thinks he's pulling a fast one when he tells me he's got a late meeting at the union hall. But whenever he does, I take off to see a movie—except that the movies I see are on the TV set in my boyfriend's apartment. Even when it's a late show, I still get home before Ron does. So I always read the movie reviews, just in case he should ever ask what I've seen, which he never does."

"I've been hoping Max will have an affair now and then, so I won't feel so guilty about the ones I'm having."

"Like I figure it's different when a man plays around, 'cause it's hardly ever serious. But with a woman, it ain't the same. And you'd always worry that she might get the V.D., and pass it on to you."

"As long as it was just prostitutes, I didn't mind too much. But now he's getting involved with this cheap little bitch who handles the switchboard at his factory, and that spells trouble."

## SEX WITH PROSTITUTES _____

As one would expect, the employment of prostitutes increases as men decrease their rate of marital intercourse. Thus, middle-aged males are more regular customers than younger males, with certain variations reflecting the educational level and socioeconomic status of the men involved. Men with minimal schooling use prostitutes more frequently than college-educated men (about 60 percent to 45 percent) but they limit themselves to lower-priced streetwalkers; whereas the more affluent males tend to employ expensive call girls. Consequently, since they are generally better educated and economically more secure on a per capita basis, Jews use prostitutes less frequently than do Catholics or Protestants—and when they do, their hired mates are likely to cost as much as $100 per hour, or twice as much as a Park Avenue analyst. There are, of course, a goodly number of relatively impecunious Catholics, Protestants and Jews who use $25 quickies from so-called tenderloin districts. As one may infer from the following comments, men who patronize whores are rather reluctant to admit it, since it suggests an inability to "make it" with other women:

"I wouldn't ordinarily use one, but once in a while you get drunk with a couple of guys, and one thing leads to another."

"When you're out of town on business you sometimes get lonely and sort of horny, and pretty soon you're in the sack with some blonde you met in the bar. Anyway, it's fast and cheap and no complications."

"Why should I feel guilty about getting a little nooky that don't mean a damn to me? Just meat on the hoof and no time wasted trying to be a big Romeo."

"Occasionally you meet someone that you wine and dine at some fancy joint, and you end up with a lousy thank-you kiss. It's just a lot cheaper and easier to get yourself a call girl—even an expensive one."

"Now, me, I never use prostitutes except to entertain an out-of-town buyer. Then I'm careful to wash my shlong with plenty of green soap and maybe a pro to make double sure. 'Cause I sure wouldn't want my wife to catch a little dose of V.D."

"Whenever I can't get it up with my wife, which is pretty often these days, I get myself a hooker who knows things I wouldn't want my wife to know—and right off the bat I can feel the old juices flowing. It's like being a new man, even if it costs a little."

All of which brings to mind the young mathematician who solemnly claimed that he had devised an equation that could accurately yield the "virility quotient" of any male respondent. Having no grasp of any mathematics beyond simple algebra, I couldn't possibly follow the twists and turns of his complex reasoning, much of which dealt with the x factor of money as an erotic variable. But with the caveat that he was probably putting me on, I submit herewith a copy of his purported equation "as it relates to a middle-aged divorced mortician who is trying to seduce a WASP widow with two minor children and a residual inherited interest in a family-owned dress shop":

$$\frac{a\sqrt{3}\times}{7\,ABY} \times (YZ^2) + MO = VQ$$

When Henry Kissinger smugly remarked that "power is the ultimate aphrodisiac," he was no doubt considering money as an integral element of power. That being the case, his long-time patron Nelson Rockefeller would have a "virility quotient" of 100 plus. And the VQ of any Saudi Arabian prince would require a new equation. But one wonders if there is a defiant genital variable that simply nullifies any kind of calculus.

## SEX AND THE SENIOR CITIZEN _____

Although sexual activity diminishes rapidly for most people as they approach and go beyond sixty years of age, there are some men and women who remain sexually active in spite of a physical decline in all other respects. My data, which generally affirm the findings of Dr. Kinsey, show that 14 percent of elderly Jewish males and 11 percent of gentile males engage in frequent or moderate intercourse. For elderly females, the percentages are slightly lower—about 11 percent for Jewish women and 9 percent for gentile women. Interestingly enough, 56 percent of Jewish male respondents and 65 percent of gentile respondents reported having "no sex" after the age of sixty; but the usual "brag factor" may account for the difference. Among females, Jewish and gentile senior citizens have an identical "no sex" percentage—a surprisingly low 46 percent for both groups. This may mean that some of the males are having sexual relations with more than one woman—or that some of these elderly women are finding younger men.

## "LIVING TOGETHER"
## ON SOCIAL SECURITY_____

One of the more interesting developments in the sexual behavior of senior citizens is the increasing number of unmarried people who live together for fiscal convenience. Thousands of elderly widows and widowers would like to remarry, but resist doing so because they would no longer be entitled to the residual Social Security benefits of their deceased spouses. Consequently, they move into the apartments of their sixty-five-year-old boyfriends or girl friends and set up housekeeping like any ordinary married couple—but many of them do so with considerable trepidation:

"Every time my son comes to visit, I have to ask Sam to move out for a few days, which he spends with his cousin Sadie. But if my son should find out I was shacking up, he'd have maybe a hemorrhage.

Now my daughter, she would understand. But my son expects me to be virgin."

"There's no question it's cheaper to live two together. And I like to cook for a man that likes good food. But I'd like to be married with him. Then I wouldn't feel so funny about the sex part. This way I still feel like I'm a chippy, with gray hair yet, and seven grandchildren."

"Listen, I wouldn't have it any other way. I don't have to live by myself, and once in a while I get a little sex. And if he starts to bore me, I just give him the walking papers."

"The best part for me is eating home-cooked meals again. That restaurant food was ruining my stomach. Also, I get to snuggle a warm body. And even without sex, that's not so bad."

"For me, the real worry part is my children finding out. This living in sin with a man—even a nice respectable dentist like Jerry—would shock them. So I keep telling them, 'Let me know in advance when you're coming.' God forbid, they should come unexpected and find us in bed together."

"Look, my children already know and they approve completely. It's a lot more convenient any way you look at it."

"Like my son says, this Social Security law is creating a bunch of gray-haired fornicators. People should be able to get married and live legal together—not like lovers in mortal sin. So he's going to ask his senator to pass some kind of new law. I think Kennedy would be the best one to ask. He knows about that kind of problem."

"My priest keeps telling me that I should give up my idea of living with this nice man I met. He says it's better to marry and give up the Social Security. But what do priests know about real life? I'm sorry I told him, and I'm wondering if going to confession means telling everything—even things you're just thinking about. At my age I can't stand all the confusion of it."

As one may gather from the foregoing comments, the daughters of such elderly people are much more liberal than the sons with respect to the out-of-wedlock liaisons of their widowed parents. The data show that 80 percent of female respondents would approve or at least accept such arrangements, whereas only 45 percent of male interviewees would respond accordingly. And among the females, Jewish women would be slightly more inclined to approve than either Catholics or WASPs (85 percent to 77 percent). But among the males, Jewish men are just as disapproving as their WASP and Catholic peers.

Most of these nonmarried couples live in areas heavily populated by retired elderly persons, usually quite distant from their former homes and conveniently removed from their adult children. Florida, Arizona and California provide the most likely havens for such arrangements—and, from purely offhand observations, one would guess that Jews are more apt to adopt this *modus vivendi* than gentiles, probably because Catholics and Protestants seem to be less numerous (on a per capita basis) in such retirement enclaves. They might also be more inhibited and less secure in their defiance of social mores.

## AGE AS A FACTOR IN MASTURBATION AND NOCTURNAL EMISSIONS

Along with the aforementioned general decline in sexual activity, there is a steep drop in the percentage of men and women who engage in masturbation after the age of sixty. My data indicate that less than 5 percent of the male population are involved in this type of erotic release, while a slightly higher 8 percent of the female population continues masturbation after that age. The Hite Report shows a much higher percentage for such elderly women, but there is reason to believe that her sample may be skewed to support a strongly held thesis. In any event, there is no apparent difference between Jews and gentiles in this regard. Nor are there any measurable variations with respect to nocturnal emissions, which are experienced by less than 4 or 5 percent of any of these groups.

## AGE AS A FACTOR IN FANTASIZING

Nevertheless, my accumulated data on "erotic fantasizing" reveal a marked difference between Jews and gentiles of both sexes. About 68 percent of Jewish respondents over the age of sixty (with no significant difference as to gender) admitted having fairly frequent fantasies. Once again, one may argue that this statistical disparity merely reflects less inhibited verbalization by the Jewish interviewees, but one could also argue that

Jews are simply more imaginative and thus inclined to fantasize about all kinds of things—including sex. One may draw whatever conclusions one wishes from some of their comments:

"So the other night I was having a dream about Sophia Loren, and I guess I started calling her name 'cause my wife shook me awake and asked 'Who's this Sophie you're talking to?' And when I told her it was Sophia Loren, she said, 'Why can't you dream someone like Grace Kelly.' So I tried, but I got only Sophia."

"The dream I keep having—twice a week maybe—is about the same woman, who worked for me ten years. But I keep worrying some day I'll say her name in my sleep and Paula will hear me. And that would be awful, 'cause she hated that girl, couldn't stand the sight of her."

"With me it's always Paul Newman. For a while I got John Lindsay in there; but he was such a lousy mayor, I couldn't stand him anymore. I even dreamed he had sex with this colored woman, and that finished him, as far as I'm concerned."

"For a long time my dream man was Frank Sinatra, but when I found out he wore a wig I switched to Elvis Presley—then it was Bronson."

"Listen, you can have your movie stars. With me, I'd rather have this waitress at my regular coffee shop. So that's who I dream about, 'cause I figure she's a real possibility—even though I ain't made my move yet. You gotta wait for the right time."

"I used to have wet dreams before I was sixty, but now they're all dry. I don't even get close to the women I dream about. They're always way out of reach."

"At my age there ain't much you can do but dream. So mostly I dream about money, about me suddenly hitting the jackpot on a lottery. Then I can dream about women—when I can really afford it."

"I used to tell my dreams to this analyst, but he kept hinting that I was really screwing my mother. So I quit going to the bastard. Who needs that kinda crap at my age."

"When I was younger, my fantasies were sharp and clear and the women were great. But lately I get nothing but smudgy images and the women are so vague I can barely see them."

"If I try real hard, I can dream about any man I want. I even had sex with Robert Redford, Jack Nicholson, Woody Allen, and the elevator operator in one single dream. But I woke up so tired I couldn't even take a bath for a while. It's lucky I don't have to confess all this stuff to my priest. He'd make me say a thousand Hail Marys."

"It's my old boyfriend I keep dreaming about, but not as much now as before. We were going to be married forty years ago, but we had this silly argument and we both married other people. Anyway, he owns a garage now, and I keep dreaming that he's fixing my carburetor. That's all he does in this dream—he fixes my carburetor."

Freudian analysts might interpret these fantasies in various ways, some more fanciful than others, but my only function is to offer a limited random sample of what I heard from my older respondents. Suffice it to say that some of these elderly men and women seemed anxious, befuddled and/or rather wistful when they spoke of their dream life.

# Occupation & Sex

*By early adolescence, the boys from class 4 homes who are destined to reach class 7 may already be identified by their high frequencies of masturbation and by their very low frequencies of intercourse.*

—Dr. Alfred Kinsey

The correlation of social class and sexual mores was a major theme of Alfred Kinsey's monumental studies of the erotic behavior of male and female Americans. Indeed, Dr. Kinsey and his colleagues went so far as to suggest that certain lower-class adolescents subconsciously pattern their early sex behavior to fit future occupational expectations. While generally confirming some of these premises, my survey goes one step further in suggesting ethnic background as a possibly important variable, which, incidentally, received only minimal consideration in the Kinsey study. But since ethnicity is often a major determinant in social and occupational mobility, it may be difficult to determine which of these factors has the greater impact on the sex life of any particular individual.

In any event, as we consider erotic behavior within several different occupations, it might be useful to bear in mind the following excerpt from Kinsey's initial survey:

*Indeed, the class 4 males who ultimately arrive at class 7 have the most restrained sociosexual histories in this whole group, and depend upon masturbation more exclusively than the class 7 males who are derived from any other parental background. It is as though the bigger the move which the boy makes between his parental class and the class toward which he aims, the more strict he is about lining up his sexual history with the pattern of the group into which he is going to move. If this were done consciously, it would be more understandable; but considering that the boy in actuality knows very little about the sexual behavior of the social group into which he is moving, it is all the more remarkable to find that these patterns are laid down at such an early age.*

## SEX HABITS OF THE WORKING CLASS———————

Among common laborers and semiskilled workers, there is a high percentage of males who have intercourse quite frequently during their teenage years and early adulthood, but they are less apt to engage in "petting to climax" or masturbation than males in higher-income occupations. Yet, curiously enough, homosexuality within this working-class group is 5 or 6 times more frequent than within business or professional groups. Jews are less numerous than gentiles at this occupational level (on a per capita basis), but even those who are laborers and semiskilled workers tend to differ from their gentile peers in that they have a lower rate of premarital intercourse but nevertheless shun frequent masturbation. Commenting on this statistical anomaly, a New York therapist told me "that they may not screw as much, but they fantasize a lot more."

The wives and daughters of working-class males seem to follow the same patterns of erotic activity—but, according to the Hite Report, the females in this group engage in masturbation much more frequently than their menfolk. In this regard, my data show no difference between gentile and Jewish females, except that Orthodox Jewish women experience longer periods of sexual abstinence due to religious strictures against intercourse during menstruation and seven days after.

## SEX HABITS OF SKILLED LABORERS———————

The sexual profile of skilled workers is measurably different. As compared with the aforementioned laborers, they fornicate less and masturbate more, but the decrease-increase is probably less than 10 percent in either case.

As one might expect, the wives, lovers and daughters of skilled workers have similar sexual behavior, but, here again, the Hite Report concludes that such women engage in masturbation much more frequently than males within their own social group. Although my data do not substantiate that claim, I must acknowledge an occasional hint of reticence on the part of some of our interviewees.

## SEX HABITS OF WHITE-COLLAR WORKERS

White-collar workers, many of whom are upwardly mobile, adhere to patterns of sexual behavior which seem to offer a balance between two extremes: They neither fornicate as frequently as laborers, nor masturbate as often as doctors and lawyers. This was particularly true when Kinsey conducted his survey, but with the "new morality" made possible by the Pill and other contraceptive devices, there has been a marked increase in intercourse among white-collar workers and a corresponding decline in masturbatory release for both males and females. There has also been a drop in "petting to climax" among younger adults. Quite obviously, the prior restrictions on "going all the way" were prompted by economic rather than moral considerations: men and women on the upward move logically assume that early parenthood impedes occupational progress.

Jewish females, particularly those interested in careers outside the home, have been especially leery of premarital intercourse. The Pill has lessened some of their worries, but my data show they are still more reluctant than gentiles. Within the latter category, Catholic women are more resistant than Protestants, mostly because of the Church's ban on abortions. As one of them wistfully commented, "Neither pills nor diaphragms are completely safe—and with my kind of memory, the rhythm method is just Vatican roulette." Female clerical workers who live outside the parental home and/or away from their hometowns—particularly those who move to large metropolitan areas—generally adopt much more liberal sex mores than those who stay home. Their after-work hunting grounds are usually singles bars, bowling alleys, church socials and such, with Jewish men and women often extending the search to museums, art exhibits, concerts, synagogue social hours and weekends in Catskill resorts.

But, as one disappointed secretary remarked after a three-day spree at Grossinger's, "The only men I met were clerks, insurance salesmen, computer technicians, passport photographers, bookbinders, cab dispatchers, an apprentice cantor, two welfare workers and a bearded private detective—and most of them hinting they were something more professional, like a lay analyst, with the accent on the lay."

## SEX AND THE SEMIPROFESSIONAL

At the semiprofessional level (schoolteachers, social workers, hospital managers, stock analysts and so on), sexual behavior becomes more constrained and often anxiety-ridden. Teachers are often ambivalent about their sexuality, occasionally getting involved in passionate affairs, then suddenly disavowing any interest in sex. And even among those who are married, these fluctuations persist. These periodic shifts may reflect ambivalent attitudes toward their pupils, their surrogate children, with a consequent unconscious rejection of parenthood, with all its erotic preambles.

Since, on a per capita basis, Jewish men and women outnumber gentiles in the teaching professions, they are particularly susceptible to this pendulum syndrome. They also may be more emotionally involved in their tutorial obligations, as evidenced by the weary reactions of a fourth-grade Anglo teacher in a Los Angeles barrio: "I really love my little Chicanos, but when they start acting up, my whole system goes to pot. I mean I can't even think of having sex with my husband when I've had a tough day at school. I won't even let him touch me."

Occasionally, a teacher will become sexually involved with one of her male students, as in the case of a thirty-three-year-old woman who initiated a precocious fourteen-year-old Puerto Rican and eventually became pregnant by him. Freely admitting the affair to one of her colleagues (who recommended an abortionist in San Juan), the teacher solemnly explained that she was merely "hoping to expand Armando's world."

The erotic behavior of social workers is also heavily influenced by the kind of work they do. With their constant exposure to the poor and the downtrodden—drug addicts, unwed mothers, unemployable neurotics, overburdened housewives, homeless children—many of them suffer from the same pendulum syndrome that afflicts schoolteachers. When one is constantly faced with fouled-up human relations, it is sometimes difficult to believe that any personal involvements are viable and worthwhile. Consequently, less than 30 percent of the social workers I interviewed were optimistic about the possibility of love and/or healthy sexual liaisons.

A considerable percentage of social workers in metropolitan areas are Jewish, but there is an increasing number of blacks, Puerto Ricans and Chicanos. Speculating on the disproportionate number of Jews in this particular field, an elderly therapist once remarked, "With our sense of gloom, it's a perfect profession. Suffering we're good at—past masters, in fact. And if you want to see the ultimate in sexual depression, my friend, just match a female social worker with one of her male colleagues. By the time they get through discussing their latest problems at some clinic or welfare center, not even Masters and Johnson could make them have sex."

For some, however, sex serves as an antidepressant. A thirty-year-old New York social worker told me that her daily contact with disturbed people made her feel better about her own self. "Like I feel more together when I compare myself with them, especially the ones whose sex lives are disastrous. So that when I get in bed with my man, each orgasm is like a thousand happy pills. And when you get that feeling, nothing can depress you." But when I saw her two days later, she was in a cloud of gloom. "It's my man who's got me down," she said. "He's into his black power thing, which means he's treating me like I'm one of his white enemies."

Black-white relationships are not uncommon among social workers, who are often drawn into that occupation by liberal humanitarian impulses that encompass racial integration as a much-desired goal. But in recent years black women have become increasingly resentful of white women who have affairs with black men. "Less than ten percent of the people in our profession are males, and only a small portion of that piddling ten percent are black, and some of them are gay or switch-hitters," one of them understandably complained. "And then all these honkie bitches take most of them. Even the ugly sloppy ones get themselves a black dude."

There is no comparable sexual integration between white

men and black women, the reverse ratio probably approxima-
ting 1 to 20 or perhaps less. My data indicate that fewer than 1
percent of white male social workers engage in such relationships, whereas 20 to 25 percent of the female social workers
have had at least one such involvement, however transitory it
may have been.

Aside from conventional intercourse, a high percentage
of social workers have frequent quasi-erotic fantasies and
dreams, and much of their fantasizing is about money and
power, with sex providing a mere backdrop for the focal action.
About 75 percent of the people I interviewed reported recur-
ring dreams about sudden wealth or increased authority on
their jobs, one of them wistfully theorizing, "Of course we fantasize about such things. What would you expect of low-paid,
powerless bureaucrats, which most of us are in the final
analysis? But even in our dreams, we have no trust in our personal skills to make money. We either win the lottery or marry a
rich shiksa who's got a letch for social workers from Brooklyn."

Such despairing humor will occasionally (perhaps inevitably) affect the sexual performance of intended lovers, who
may find themselves involved in dispirited but desperately patient foreplay. "Listen," one man told us, "when I'm in that kind
of mood, I'm too worried about not getting an erection to concern myself with what's happening to her you-know-what."
And from the feminine side, this comment: "The way I've been
feeling lately, I've almost given up hope that I'll get any satisfaction from sex—clitoral or otherwise. I just don't think my husband can handle it, not with the kind of worries he's got about
himself."

## SEX HABITS OF PROFESSIONALS

One might assume that supposedly secure professionals (doctors, lawyers, dentists, professors and such) generally enjoy
more satisfying sex lives than those who have a lower occupational status, but, in some instances, their economic security is
overshadowed by lingering, often debilitating psychic inse-
curities. For example, I was told by three female psychoanalysts
that most male analysts are "miserable and incompetent
lovers"—even those who apparently are quite successful in

treating patients with severe sexual problems. Prompted by such perhaps-biased speculations, I subsequently conducted short interviews with ten male analysts (eleven others politely declined) to ascertain how they felt about their own sexuality and about that of their female colleagues.*

One of them freely admitted that he was a "lousy" lover, and quickly added, "but only when I'm trying to lay a female analyst, and that's because they always try to analyze why you prefer one position over another." He went on to say that he had always enjoyed successful relations with nonprofessional women, including some of his patients.

Although some analysts and psychoanalysts take advantage of the powerful "transference" that takes place between doctor and patient, my data suggest that less than 15 percent of said analysts admit to indulging in this type of unprofessional conduct. And, with the recent court actions against a prominent New York psychiatrist, that small percentage has probably diminished (at least temporarily) to a near zero. Commenting on this much-publicized lawsuit, one of the psychiatrist's colleagues told me that he had never taken advantage of a patient and quite frequently had resisted sexual advances from both female and male patients. "Some of my newer people have been tempting—particularly the young wife of my favorite nephew—but most of my older patients have lost any appeal they may have had at the beginning. There's nothing more boring than a woman whose psyche has become as familiar as an old wart."

According to this line of reasoning, gynecologists would be prime candidates for sexual apathy, but, judging from various comments by some of my female interviewees about their gynecologist husbands or lovers, many of them manage to retain a lively interest in sex despite their continuous exposure to the female genitalia.

Some, of course, do become coldly clinical and completely detached, so that sex is nothing more than a mechanical exercise utterly devoid of any emotion. There is, however, at least one gynecologist who is far from indifferent to sex, who,

---

*Since I had initially planned an article on the sexual behavior of professionals, I also interviewed twenty-five laywers and twenty-two doctors in addition to the few already included in my 722 interviews.

in fact, despises anything that detracts from what he calls "natural intercourse." He is especially peevish about diaphragms. "Because when my girl friend—this psychiatric nurse—comes to my office after the day shift, I'm all ready to pounce her. But then she has to run into the goddamn bathroom to put on her lousy diaphragm, and by the time she gets back, I've lost my damned erection." When asked why she doesn't insert it in advance, he said, "Hell, I've told her to do that! But she never does. So I'm beginning to think that she gets her rocks off by making me wait."

Needless to say, sexual intercourse between doctors and nurses (or patients) is a common experience. My statistics show that at least 65 percent of the medical profession engage in extracurricular sex on a fairly regular basis. Dentists are included in this category, but it should be noted that many of them are so phobic about oral bacteria that they adamantly refuse to French kiss a potential bedmate, even if it means losing her. One of my interviewees angrily remembered slapping her orthodontist's face when he handed her a paper cup of Lavoris and asked her to gargle just as she was about to crawl into bed with him. "So I threw it in his eyes and told him to get out—except that it was *his* apartment. So I got out and didn't even bother to put on my girdle, I was so damned mad."

Lawyers are much less likely to have a bacterial phobia, but many have been accused of an oral affliction we might call "argumentaphilia"—that is, a compulsion to argue the pros and cons of any conceivable subject—which is often an impediment to erotic enterprise. As one woman expressed it, "No matter what kind of sex I suggest, my husband insists on presenting well-reasoned, lawyerly arguments for some other position. So I finally get bored and turn on Johnny Carson, which is probably what my husband wanted in the first place."

Offhand, one would guess that she is married to an appellate lawyer or corporate counsel, a man who deals with legal documents more often than with people. Had she been married to a trial lawyer, whose principal concern is with people rather than things, she might get a different response—though not necessarily. In any event, criminal and civil trial lawyers are often considered more sexually active than "office laywers," probably because they have many more female clients and also have direct access to female jurors, many of whom develop crushes on the usually flamboyant charmers who specialize in jury cases.

One notoriously successful California lawyer once boasted that he had dated at least one juror from every case he had ever tried, "and I've laid at least fifty percent of them." An equally boastful Texas divorce lawyer told me that he had seduced "no less than thirty-three percent of my female clients during the past twenty years—except for one three-month period when I was recovering from a hemorrhoid operation." Smiling broadly and nudging my elbow, he added that each of his seductions was considered "my Texas fee, which I don't have to declare on my income tax." Indeed, the term "Texas fee" is widely used among trial lawyers in the Southwest.

Although it would be difficult to distinguish between boast and fact, my findings suggest that at least 60 percent of trial lawyers engage in extramarital affairs, as compared with 35 percent for the profession as a whole. Since women still constitute only a small percentage of the total number of practicing attorneys, I won't hazard a guess as to their sexual behavior.

With respect to ethnic differences in the sex lives of psychoanalysts, medical doctors, dentists, lawyers and other professionals, one should bear in mind that Jews are heavily represented in each of these professions, considerably beyond their numerical proportion (about 6 or 7%) of the national population. Consequently, their sexual behavior generally reflects the norms of their respective occupations, although they would appear to be more liberal (or less up-tight) with respect to new and experimental modes of sexual release.

As for the wives of these professional men, they seem to follow the same erotic life-styles as their husbands, except that some of them seem to be actively involved in adulterous affairs of a more serious nature than the so-called matinée trysts in which their husbands participate. A few of their random comments may shed some light on their attitudes toward marriage and sex:

"I know that my husband spends his golf afternoons at some local motel with some little chippy from the hospital, but I just can't cheapen myself that way. If I'm going to fool around, I'll go to Palm Springs or some other nice resort where you can meet someone decent and refined."

"My husband keeps reminding me that I was also a nurse—but I was a lot different than this cheap little bitch who works at his clinic. I guess I shouldn't worry about her, but he's at that dumb dangerous stage, when sex can turn any man's head into mush."

"When I first met my husband, I was a juror in one of his cases, so I know how he operates. But even though I sit in the courtroom during most of his trials, pretending that I'm still thrilled by his cheesy tactics, I'm sure that he's having affairs with some of his dumb wide-eyed jurors who seem to dig all his crap."

"I don't think my husband screws anyone but his clients, and I don't mean *sexual* screwing. He's too damned busy for that."

"When I first found out that he was fooling around with other women, I was really crushed. But then I decided to find myself a lover, which was pretty easy—so now I don't care what he does . . . or with whom."

"My only worry is that he'll pick up a case of V.D. and pass it on to me. But since we have sex only once a month (or maybe less), the chances are fairly remote."

"I once dated this doctor who was an X-ray specialist, and he was always saying I had beautiful bones. And whenever he played with my fanny, he used to say, 'You've got a great *caudus equina*.' He even wrote it down for me. Then one night I asked him what those words really meant, and he started giggling and laughing and almost choked before he could tell me. 'Well, first of all,' he said, '*caudus* means tail and *equina* means horse—so the last three bones of your spine are called horse's tail.' Well, I tried to laugh it off, but I knew he was putting me down—that I was just an animal to him. So I finally stopped dating him."

"My gynecologist tried to put the make on me, but I turned him down because I had this feeling that he knew too much about me. After all, when a man has looked down your you-know-what, there isn't much mystery left."

Despite this particular woman's negative reaction, there are many women who think gynecologists are extremely attractive. In fact, more than 30 percent of my female interviewees have had occasional fantasies about their gynecologists, most of which included some form of erotic interplay between doctor and patient. But one woman had several dreams in which her doctor and her plumber were fused into one person, and several months later, as the plumber was repairing her garbage disposal, she called him "Dr. Manion," then quickly tried to cover her embarrassment by telling him that he had the delicate hands of a gynecologist, and was further embarrassed when he asked her, "What's a gynecologist?" Understandably flustered by the question, she mumbled something vague about internal medicine and backed out of the kitchen. "He must of thought I was a real looney," she added, "because he obviously knew that his hands weren't at all delicate. Yet he somehow reminded me of my doctor, but I can't say why."

## SEX HABITS OF ARTISTS AND ENTERTAINERS

Since they are inherently more creative than most people, artists and entertainers generally have more expansive sex habits than lawyers, doctors, dentists and other professionals, but, because of the periodic uncertainty of any creative endeavor, they are also susceptible to periods of sexual malaise induced by occupational anxiety. For example, a novelist may suddenly encounter a "writer's block," which often leads to a drastic change in his sexual behavior—perhaps a temporary impotency which may last as long as his inability to write. One can only speculate about the erotic impasses that may have been caused by Katherine Anne Porter's twenty-year struggle to produce *Ship of Fools*, or Joseph Heller's twelve-year ordeal with *Something Happened*, or Ralph Ellison's endless effort to finish his still-to-be-published and much-awaited second novel.

Looking at the writer's block from a different perspective, Norman Mailer has flatly stated that "every fuck is a lost page," which may be an easy out for someone afflicted by psychic drains totally unrelated to sex. But one cannot dismiss the damaging effects of certain unhappy and unhealthy relationships which may cost a writer not only pages, but whole chapters. As one psychiatrist recently said, "It's not the act of intercourse that drains the creative juices—it's all the negative conflicts that sometimes accompany sex which cause the trouble. Intercourse in itself may actually restore creative energy, but not when it's preceded or followed by prolonged anger and anxiety and endless recriminations and spasms of doubt that leave both parties in a state of utter exhaustion. So, Mailer is sadly mistaken, or putting us on, when he equates a spurt of semen with a page of fiction."

On the other hand, there are those who feel that sexual and/or marital failure sharpens and increases a writer's perception of human nature. In this regard, it is interesting to note that Mailer and Saul Bellow each have been married and divorced several times. They are also Jews and thus presumably susceptible to the ethnic pressures and advantages of their Judaic heritage. One should also note that both of them are considered male chauvinists by most feminist writers, many of whom are also Jewish and thus keenly conscious of the male imperatives of their ancient religion. Indeed, there is a large number of successful Jewish writers (here again, the percentage is three or four times larger than the proportion of Jews in the general population) and many of them also qualify as male chauvinists, particularly those who have capitalized on the apparent popularity of novels which feature amusing but denigrating portrayals of Jewish Princesses and Jewish mothers. But as one female critic commented, "I'm getting tired of reading 400-page insults by petulant men who started hating women when they suddenly realized that they would never be able to marry their own mothers."

Apparently, her view is not shared by most of the women I interviewed during the past six years, 80 percent of whom expressed very positive feelings about Mailer, Bellow, Roth, Malamud, Heller, Salinger, Wouk, Kazan, Greenburg, Epstein, Ginsberg, Tallmer, Gelber, Selby, and Larner. They also enjoyed such female writers as Lillian Hellman, Erica Jong, Renata Adler, Lois Gould and Vivian Gornick. Several of them highly approved the uninhibited, deliciously lewd and funny descriptions of Jong's heroine in *Fear of Flying* as she pursued the apparently unattainable "zipless fuck," and they were particularly pleased by her vastly amusing put-downs of every man she met. "Jong is our answer to Roth," one of them said with a hint of shared triumph. "And I'll bet you men really hate her."

The so-called battle of the sexes may be less apparent in other art forms, but the conflict is always there. Actors and actresses are forever vying for attention on stage or screen, often employing subtle and sneaky ploys to upstage each other, and prima ballerinas often find themselves competing with male dancers, even though the ballet, in particular, essentially stars the female. In any event, the artists' very obvious narcissism all too frequently nullifies any chance for what is called "normal" sex between partners of opposite genders. Consequently, there is more than the usual amount of homosexuality or autosexuality (what else would one call self-love?) in the performing arts, and many of the male-female liaisons that do exist (with or without marriage) are extended acts of sado-masochism with unwanted children serving as helpless spectators.

There are, of course, a certain number of successful marriages among actors, dancers and musicians, but the degree of sexual harmony within these marriages is often dependent on the degree of artistic success by either or both spouses. "When my career takes a dive," says a Hollywood actor, "my sex life is nil. Not even Raquel Welch could turn me on—much less my wife." And a moderately famous screen actress once told a friend, "When things go wrong at the studio, I'm an absolute zombie in bed. In fact, I can't stand to be touched by either my husband or my lover." Somewhat in the same vein, a homosexual dancer wearily confessed to his analyst, "I'm a terrible bitch when my dancing goes stale. I'll even flirt with some stupid straight john just to rile my lover. And believe me, darling, he's easy to rile."

Interestingly enough, stand-up comedians—even the most successful ones—seem to have more fragile libidos than other stage performers, perhaps because they so continuously deprecate themselves, sometimes masochistically à la Lenny Bruce and Shelley Berman, or in the more endearing and wistful manner of Woody Allen and the late Jack Benny. But whatever technique they use, the core of their humor is apt to be sexual frustration and/or defeat, with the comedian himself in the loser's role. Once in a while, the more hostile comics (like Don Rickles) vent their ill-disguised resentment of women with cheap shots at their wives or any unlucky woman in the audience.

As one glances at the names mentioned above, one must

inevitably realize that most of our successful comedians are Jewish, as are the men and women who write their material, much of which reflects the irony and skepticism of a people who have survived great emotional hardships through the medium of humor.

## SEX HABITS OF POLITICIANS

For anyone who has been involved in politics, whether on a local or national level, the political sex scandals of 1976 hardly merited a half-raised eyebrow. As Lyndon Johnson's brother has often said, "The only surprise is getting caught, especially here in Washington, where adultery is a lot more common than legislation—and much more interesting." Indeed, according to Sam Houston Johnson, there is no level of government that is free of extramarital philandering, from the Supreme Court to the lowest echelon of the Civil Service. But congressmen are probably the most active miscreants, certainly the most notorious. One knowledgeable observer of Capitol Hill has estimated that 60 percent of our senators and 75 percent of our representatives have been involved in sexual relations with women other than their wives, which may account for the drag-foot reluctance of Congress to investigate Representatives Wayne Hayes and Wilbur Mills.

The same high percentages would no doubt apply to elected officials in the state houses and local city councils, all of which brings to mind the rueful comment of a California woman whose husband asked for a divorce so that he could marry his flashy blonde campaign manager: "We wives don't stand a chance, with all these political groupies who hang around a candidate, volunteering their services and themselves, and making him think that he's God's gift to humanity. What stronger aphrodisiac is there than the idolatry of a younger woman, especially if a man thinks his wife is an aging nag. But that's how I got him, except that he was a young professor and I was the worshipful student."

Her reference to groupies is an apt one: Political office seekers are indeed surrounded by female volunteers of all ages, some of them bored or disillusioned housewives looking for outside distractions. Many, of course, are idealists hoping to further some cause, but quite often the cause becomes embodied in the candidate they are working for, so that he is idealized even beyond his own narcissistic image of himself. Consequently, as the continuous proximity of candidate and campaign worker evolves into intimacy, with both of them away from home for extended periods, sexual involvement seems almost inevitable. Since divorce is still considered damaging to a political career in most of the country, the successful candidate generally stays married but nevertheless takes his lover to Washington or the state capital, where she becomes a well-paid member of his staff, irrespective of her administrative or secretarial skills. And there she will remain, faithfully attending to his every need and serving as his hostess for office parties his wife can't (or won't) attend, yet always fretting about some future election when he'll meet a younger and more fervent groupie who may know newer and more novel ways to satisfy his occupational narcissism. Several of my 722 interviewees were actively engaged in politics, and their comments on the sexual behavior of politicians were most enlightening:

"I wasn't hired to type."

"My wife never realized how valuable Hildy was in my campaign. She arranged all my appointments, my hotel reservations, my travel arrangements, and kept everybody happy—including me. But the sex part was only incidental."

"My husband claimed she was a good campaign worker, but all she did was serve his coffee and rub his feet and God knows what else when they went out of town. Well, now she's his administrative assistant, earning twenty thousand dollars a year and not doing a thing except rubbing his feet and occasionally answering the phone with that silly sexy voice."

"It's really hard to work with someone who's shacking up with the boss. I mean she does some really dumb things that could really alienate a few constituents. But you don't dare criticize her, because she's really got that old bastard by the balls."

"I know his wife and everybody else thought I was just a sexpot, but I could type as good as anyone else in the office—even though my spelling wasn't all that perfect."

"Well, Joanie may not be able to spell 'cat,' mind you, but she knows a lotta other things that are more important."

# 7
# Social Level & Sex

Although the so-called sexual revolution of the 1960s affected the life-styles of thousands of young people in this country and abroad, particularly middle-class college students, most adult Americans seemed to follow the same sexual patterns that Kinsey detected two decades earlier. Some were considered counterrevolutionaries and "prisoners of a lower level of consciousness" by their spaced-out children, many of whom had become instant devotees of a new orthodoxy called the drug culture. There were, of course, a few middle-aged parents who discarded their conventional clothes and hair styles, hoping to fraternize with the generally exclusionary youth cult—and, when refused admission, tried desperately to emulate their speech, their manner and their attitude. More often than not, their imitations were embarrassingly absurd and were inevitably resented by their children, who subconsciously wanted their parents to remain square—otherwise, what was there to rebel against?

But even those parents who maintained their traditional life-styles, who adamantly refused to go along with the use of any kind of drugs, nevertheless found themselves "going along" with their teenagers' liberated sex mores. This has been particularly true of upper- and middle-class parents, whose college-age daughters and sons started living in joint dormitories in the late 1960s, many of the girls having been previously initiated to the use of the Pill while in high school. As one suburban matron commented, "I'd rather have her sleeping around than smoking pot." "But she does both," added her less complaisant husband. "But what are you going to do?" the woman responded. "It's like that everywhere you go—even Nebraska."

As one might suspect, fathers are much more disturbed about this turn of events than their wives are; but few, if any, have gone so far as to object in the much-publicized manner of the irate father who wrote an open letter to the parents of all

Wellesley College students, strongly protesting what he called "the notoriously promiscuous conduct" of his daughter's schoolmates. One of them subsequently told a reporter that "the only man who sleeps in my room is my lover." Though a shade less candid, most other Wellesley women calmly dismissed this aggrieved father's complaint as amusingly old-fashioned. And although some of their parents probably agreed with that fatherly protest, they preferred to remain silent, no doubt sensing that it would be futile to join the protester's lonely crusade.

Had they been working-class parents—particularly Italian, Chicano, Puerto Rican or of any other Latin extraction—their reactions would have been much different. Indeed, their daughters would have been afraid to cohabit openly with any male, on or off campus. Not long ago several Chicana students at the University of California at Riverside decided to move into a new women's dormitory, but their very macho fathers instantly and unequivocally vetoed their decision, even though on-campus residence would spare their daughters a hundred-mile daily commute to their classes. "No daughter of mine is going to move out of my house until she gets married," one of the fathers emphatically told a university counselor. "Only whores live away from home." That same sentiment was recently expressed by the father of a twenty-eight-year-old Puerto Rican woman who earns $20,000 per year in an administrative position. She had once moved into her own apartment despite a raging protest from both her parents, but she soon moved back home because of her father's constant harassment. "I had given him a key to the apartment, just to calm his suspicions—but he would come by at all hours, past midnight or before dawn, and he would search under my bed and in all my closets to see if some man were there. So I finally gave up and went back to their crappy apartment."

Another glimpse of working-class sexual attitudes was offered in the motion picture *Rocky*, which features a tough Italian clubhouse boxer who makes most of his modest earnings as a thumb-busting enforcer for a Mafia bookie. Although living in a ghetto where the street language is as raw and relentlessly obscene as the gutter talk of any other poor neighborhood, Rocky gets furious when his new girl friend's brother asks if they've slept together. "What kinda dirty talk is dat?" he bellows. "You got a filthy mouth!" Later that day, Rocky lectures a tough tomboy about "not talking dirty" and hanging around a street gang, "cuz pretty soon deez guys will lose respect for ya and you'll get treated like some whore who nobody respects on accounta the way ya always talking dirty." As for Rocky's attitude toward his extremely shy and almost-spinsterish girl friend (who has lived with an older bachelor brother since their parents' deaths), one gets the impression that he will treat her like a virgin even after they have had intercourse, and that they will have sex only in the missionary position because any other position would seem perverse to Rocky. It's interesting to note that Rocky's superchaste girl was the unacceptably wild sister in *The Godfather*, another film that shows the double-standard machismo of Italian men with working-class antecedents. As Kinsey would say, even when people get rich and move into a higher echelon, whether it's the Mafia or any other socioeconomic structure, they generally keep their original notions about sex and marriage.

The examples just cited once again illustrate the curious disparity in the sexual behavior and attitudes of individuals from different social classes and ethnic backgrounds. These disparities are more readily apparent as one analyzes certain socioethnic responses to various aspects of erotic activity—petting-to-climax, nocturnal emissions, masturbation, premarital intercourse, adultery, marital intercourse, spouse-swapping, intercourse with prostitutes and homosexuality.

## PETTING TO CLIMAX

Since it means delayed gratification and a postponement of childbearing as an economic imperative, petting-to-climax is more generally practiced by middle- or upper-class youth for whom early marriage may bring an abrupt end to upward mobility. Working-class youth with similar aspirations also resort to "hot necking" as a substitute for intercourse, but they represent only a small percentage of their socioeconomic group.

But even now, with the Pill and other contraceptive devices offering considerable protection against pregnancy, intense and prolonged necking is still not as popular with the laborer's children as it is with the banker's offspring. Some low-income youth consider French kissing "too sloppy and full of germs." Others believe it's "perverted" and "dirty." Still others object to the overstimulation of deep kissing and bodily caresses, "like it makes me come before I can get a chance to hop on her for some real screwing, and she ends laughing at me on accounta all the goop on my pants." Such attitudes probably reflect parental as well as peer-group sentiments. Similarly, the more affluent and better-educated youth's willingness to neck for prolonged periods is a reflection of parental admonitions to wait for gratification. To wait and to persevere have always been key elements to economic and occupational success, and the habit of waiting and persevering may carry over to other life activities, including sex. Thus, even after years of marriage, when childbearing is no longer a central concern, middle- and upper-class men may be able to delay orgasm longer than less patient working-class males—but this, of course, is mere conjecture.

As for the wives of these men, my data indicate a general dissatisfaction with the precoital habits of males from all social levels. Working-class spouses complain that their husbands kiss very little and almost completely avoid genital stimulation. Middle-class spouses say that their husbands pet "a lot less than when we were in college" and that they engage in the wrong kind of genital stimulation, almost always assuming that the vagina is the prime area for intense titillation. The wives of upper-class businessmen and professionals voice similar complaints, also adding a poignant note about "husbands married to their jobs."

## MASTURBATION—MALE AND FEMALE

As Kinsey noted almost thirty years ago, masturbation is the most popular form of sexual release in the pre-adult stage. More than 90 percent of the male population have masturbatory experiences during their early years, but the frequency of such activity is much higher among college-educated males. Indeed, for this particular group, it is the prime source of premarital sexual outlet. More specifically, masturbation provides nearly 80 percent of their orgasms during early adolescence, as compared with 52 percent for adolescents with less than high-school education. The difference is even more marked when youngsters reach their late teens, during which higher-level males have 66 percent of their orgasms through masturbation, as compared with 30 percent for lower-level youngsters.

But these class distinctions are perhaps more striking among married males. For those with less than a high-school education, only 20 to 30 percent masturbate during their early marital years, with a slightly higher percentage for the later years of marriage. Men with high-school educations closely match the less-educated in this respect. But among married males with college and/or professional education, more than 60 to 70 percent continue to masturbate during the early and middle years of their marriages.

Although the aforementioned statistics were produced from research conducted three decades ago, our less exact data indicate no significant difference in the masturbatory habits of contemporary American males. Then, as now, with respect to occupational classes, professional men masturbate more frequently than men in lesser occupations. And this is true whether such professionals originate from a lower parental class or whether they come from parents who were also professional. This would seem to confirm Kinsey's premise that upwardly mobile persons adopt the sexual patterns of the class into which they aspire to move. The following Kinsey graph, which also generally reflects our findings, aptly illustrates the socioeconomic disparities in sexual behavior:

MASTURBATION

EDUCATIONAL
LEVEL

OCCUPATIONAL
CLASS

2

0-8                    3

9-12                   4

13+                    5

6

7

*Masturbation, by educational level and occupational class*

Kinsey's premise also seems to contradict the familiar parental admonition that "playing with yourself will make you go crazy." In any event, the distinctions between occupational classes are even more extreme than the differences between educational levels, insofar as masturbation is concerned.

As for the masturbatory activities of females, the Hite Report would have us believe that there are no class distinctions: that the workingman's wife stimulates herself as often as the doctor's wife, irrespective of what their husbands do. Judging from my necessarily limited interviews, I am inclined to believe that there are class distinctions—not as pronounced as the differences between upper- and lower-class males, but enough to be categorized as "measurably different." I would, of course, readily admit that my data may be distorted by the fact that upper-class women are less inhibited in discussing their sex habits than the shyer, less articulate wives of unskilled laborers, but the same would be true of the women who answered Ms. Hite's questionnaire. Be that as it may, the following condensed comments may give us some further insights into this particular aspect of erotic outlet:

"My husband often plays with himself when he's asleep. I guess he's dreaming about some other woman, but I can never get her name because he just mumbles and snorts and sometimes giggles as his thing gets harder and harder."

"I really don't know whether or not I masturbate in my sleep, but once in a while I wake up with a fantastic erection."

"Once in a while, when the wife ain't ready for me or when she's got the curse and I'm feeling horny, I go into the bathroom and jerk off for a few minutes. But I wouldn't want her to know that, 'cuz she'd think I'm some sort of queer that beats his own meat like some kid still in school who can't make it with anyone."

"My father, who was a doctor, used to tell me that masturbation would cause some sort of brain damage, but I managed to make Phi Beta Kappa even though I was jerking off almost every night, which was common practice in our dorm. But I didn't really believe all his crap, because I used to hear my mom tell him not to play with himself. She'd yell at him, so I couldn't help hearing her. Anyway, I guess it runs in the family."

"Sometimes I think my old lady plays with herself, 'cause she sorta smells different. But I never say nothing about it. I figure let sleeping dogs go on sleeping. What you really don't know don't matter, even though it keeps bothering you when ya start thinking that maybe you ain't got enuff to satisfy her. So it's better that ya don't know."

"I know that a priest probably has to masturbate himself so that he can keep celibate from women—at least that's what my dad used to say about them. But I could never confess to a priest that I play with my own self, 'cause women should act different. Anyway, it satisfies more than sex with a drunk husband."

"I sort of panic when I can't get it up for my wife or my girl friend. Like I'm supposed to be a stud cop. So I do a little hand pumping and that sometimes helps, and when that don't work, I put on the old snooze act."

"Whenever I feel an itch and reach down to scratch myself, my wife immediately tells me to quit playing with myself. Or she teasingly says I'm always worried about losing the family jewels."

My research suggests that Jewish males and females are more active than Protestants and Catholics with respect to petting and masturbation, but the differences are most likely related to class distinctions rather than ethnic propensity. Since, on a per capita basis, Jews have a higher percentage of well-educated and affluent individuals, their sexual behavior reflects the mores of their respective social levels. But within each of the various levels, there are no discernible differences between gentiles and Jews.

## NUDITY

It should be noted that upper-class males prefer to be naked when they have intercourse, whereas working-class men prefer to remain partially clothed. Females are generally more inhibited about having sex in the nude, but upper-class women usually accept nudity as a normal accompaniment of coitus. Consequently, about 90 percent of upper-level fornication is performed by completely nude partners, but that figure is less than 50 percent for intercourse involving persons from lower income levels. Commenting on this cultural phenomenon, Kinsey wrote: "This is one point in human sexual behavior to which arguments as to what is natural and what is unnatural have never been applied, for there can be no question of the fact that intercourse without clothing is biologically normal, and that the custom of having intercourse with clothing is a distinctly cultural acquirement."

Adhering to a similar degree of modesty, working-class couples prefer to have intercourse in the dark or with very dim lighting, whereas upper-level lovers often prefer more light, or nothing dimmer than candlelight. Here again, women seem a shade more modest at all levels, perhaps because they have been conditioned to associate nudity with immoral conduct. Some, particularly older women, may feel that their sagging breasts and bumpy, wrinkling thighs can no longer bear intense scrutiny. Several of our interviewees were quite explicit on this particular subject:

"Me and my husband would never have sex naked. I wouldn't want him to see me, and I sure don't want to see him either—not with all that hair he's got all over his body. I'd think I was doing love with an ape."

"I like plenty of light when I'm having sex, especially when some gal goes down on me and I can see exactly what's happening. That's a real turn-on, man."

"With the way my body is beginning to sag and wrinkle, I'm partial to darkness. There's no point in spoiling his illusions."

"I like my wife to wear a slinky black nightgown—like Rita Hayworth used to wear. In fact, that's who I try to imagine my wife is—Rita Hayworth. Except my imagination ain't that good."

"My husband would probably call me a whore if I ever came to bed naked. He won't even scrub my back when I'm taking a bath, 'cause he doesn't want to see me in my birthday suit."

"This man I knew when I was waitressing—he was a cop—well, anyway, he would take all his clothes off except his socks."

"I always come to bed with my panties and bra, which my husband takes off when he's ready. But he always leaves them under the sheets, so I can put them back on when we're through. That way he won't see me naked when I go to the bathroom afterwards. And he always keeps his shorts on."

"I have these black and red see-through panties, with lace over my you-know-what—which really gets him excited. But he wouldn't want me to be all naked. That's what whores do."

"My wife and I always have sex in the nude and by candlelight, preferably three or four long slender candles to give us plenty of soft light. But my secretary absolutely refuses to take off her slip and panties until she's under the sheets."

# 8
# Incest &
# Other Taboos

*As everyone who cares to know knows, Lewis Carroll liked to take nude photographs of little girls. Until recently, none of these photographs were thought to have survived, but four have now been located among the families of their subjects, and are being exhibited at the Rosenbach Foundation Museum in Philadelphia. All four pictures have been hand-colored and painted over, so they do not accurately represent Carroll's original work, but nevertheless remain interesting documents in the history of Victorian sexuality, Carroll's in particular.*

*They are not interesting in quite the obvious way, however. Carroll's lifetime fascination with little girls, and his photography studies, have sometimes been dealt with as his dirty little secret. But it wasn't a secret—the girls' parents were Carroll's acquaintances and colleagues at Oxford; they consented to the sessions and were often present at the time. Nor did the parties involved think it was dirty—many Victorians thought, following Wordsworth, that little children were innocent imps of God. They were frequently allowed to go naked on hot days, especially at the beach.*

*In a monograph on the pictures, Carroll scholar Morton N. Cohen disclaims any suggestion of prurience on Carroll's part. Not all modern observers are likely to agree. But odd as Carroll was, it may be even odder that only a century ago a man whose sexual repression was apparently total, nevertheless did important work in mathematics, wrote "Alice in Wonderland," enjoyed good health, had a lot of friends and a good time, and was considered socially acceptable and as sane as the next fellow.*

—Hilton Kramer, *The New York Times*

*There are some psychoanalysts who contend that they have never had a patient who has not had incestuous relations; but such a statement is totally out of line with the specific records which have been obtained in this study or which, for that matter, have been obtained in any other survey of the general population.*

—Dr. Alfred C. Kinsey

In asserting that the aforementioned psychoanalysts are "totally out of line," Dr. Kinsey apparently failed to note that the analysts were obviously talking about their own patients, a fairly limited number of people who have felt compelled to seek help because of certain highly disturbing emotional conflicts. If the analyst is a conventional Freudian, one would expect an intense probing of the Oedipal matrix. But I think Kinsey is needlessly cautionary when he suggests that "the clinician must beware that the select group of persons who come to a clinic does not color his thinking concerning the population as a whole."

Since Kinsey's monumental study devoted only one paragraph in 765 pages to the subject of incest, one must assume that his researchers were inordinately shy or were confronted with massive reticence on the part of the people they interviewed. Thus, Kinsey came to the unequivocal conclusion that heterosexual incest occurs more frequently in the thinking of clinicians and social workers than it does in actual performance. But if one is to believe such writers as William Faulkner, Flannery O'Connor, Erskine Caldwell, Carson McCullers, James Dickey and Wright Morris—all of whom are perceptive and stubbornly honest observers of the social mores of certain rural sections of this country—one might conclude that incest is more prevalent than some people are willing to believe. Or perhaps it is merely more dramatic for literary purposes and thus gets more attention than is warranted in a strictly statistical sense. (A friend of mine, herself a Southerner, is firmly convinced that the rural South has the highest rate of incest in the nation. To emphasize her point, she reminded me of the Southerner's satiric definition of a virgin: "Any twelve-year-old girl who can run faster than her father . . . or brothers.") In any event, the taboo nature of incest makes it difficult to ascertain how much of it actually occurs at any level of our society. Yet a few guarded comments from some of my interviewees, speaking obliquely about "this girl I know" or about "this guy who lived next door," have led me to suspect that they themselves were once involved in some type of incestuous relationship.

There are, of course, various levels of incestuous behavior. First of all, there is *actual* incest, which involves some type of sexual intercourse between two or more people. Secondly, there is *quasi-incest*, in which the participants mask their sexual desires with "goosing" or some other playful form of genital contact, or the prolonged embrace of father and daughter, brother and sister. Thirdly, and probably most prevalent, there is fantasy incent.

## FANTASIES OF INCESTUOUS RELATIONSHIPS _____

After interviewing several psychologists and analysts, and further reviewing the mostly veiled responses of many of our interviewees, I have come to believe that most people have (at one time or another) fantasized about having sexual contact with a mother, father, sister, brother or close relative—so that such fantasies are indeed statistically normal—but still taboo in the eyes of most people. Note, for example, the faltering evasive comments of the respondents when asked if they had ever had fantasies of incest:

"Not exactly . . . but I once dreamed that my sister and me were the only people left in the world after an atom bomb explosion. I kept calling her Eva, although her name is really Lucy. Anyway, we were on this small island and couldn't get away from it."

"I sometimes dream that my mother has died, and I take her place, cooking these fabulous gourmet dinners for my dad and fixing his martinis just the way he likes them."

"I once had this dream where my mother and me won this dance contest at Roseland, doing a tango. But my dad got mad at us, claiming it was too sexy to dance that way. Of course, he was jealous because he never could dance very well. So I was the one who danced with my mom at these family parties. But in this dream we won the top prize."

"My brother was the sexiest guy in our neighborhood, and I really had a crush on him—all through high school. Once in a while I've had this dream where I've actually married him. But it's one of those platonic marriages with no sex. I once made the mistake of telling my husband about this dream, assuming he would think it was pretty funny. And he just stared at me—with this real cold look in his eyes—and he wouldn't even touch me that night."

"Look, mister, if a man can't love his mother, who should he love? But I mean it don't have to be sexy."

"I'll have to admit that I once had a letch for my mother—especially when I was a teenager and used to watch her walking around the house in her flimsy nightgown, so that her tits were easy to see. And I've sometimes dreamed of having sex with her—but I have never touched her, never ever."

Since very few people will ever admit to participating in actual incest (or even quasi-incest), there is no way of determining any statistical difference between WASPs, Catholics and Jews in this particular aspect of sexual behavior. But my survey does indicate certain rather remarkable differences in the types of fantasies they have. For example, the incestuous fantasies of WASPs tend to concentrate on sister and brother relationships. Catholics, on the other hand, tend to fantasize about sex between fathers and daughters. And the incestuous fantasies of Jews lean toward involvements of mothers and sons. One should note, however, that the fantasies of all these groups run the gamut of all intrafamily liaisons, despite the marked tendencies just mentioned.

In any event, it is difficult to resist speculating on the reasons for such ethnic variations. Could it be that most WASPs are so sexually constrained that they can't bring themselves even to fantasize about sex between parent and child? With respect to the incest taboo in general, one might recall Hamlet's agonized breast-beating over his widowed mother's marriage to his uncle, which was nothing more than collateral incest between a woman and her brother-in-law, which in her mind probably didn't seem at all incestuous. As for Catholics, one might consider the possibility that certain fathers look upon their young daughters as the Virgin Marys they have always longed for but would never dare touch except in the most lurid fantasies. With respect to Jewish fantasies of mother-son involvements, one might theorize about the legendary domineering influence of such mothers, especially with respect to their sons. An amusingly exaggerated version of this often-publicized syndrome was presented by Elaine May and Mike Nichols in a comedy skit for Jimmy Carter's inauguration. Here we saw a future Jewish president abjectly and guiltily responding to his teary but iron-willed mother who naggingly complains that he hasn't phoned her as often as usual.

All of which brings to mind the fact that the "Jewish mother" gets more than her share of attention (and comic condemnation) because there is a disproportionately large number of Jewish writers and comedians in this country, many of whom have found a limitless fund of humor in the Oedipal conflict. Indeed, when one considers the disproportionately large number of Jewish psychologists and psychoanalysts—and the fact that many of their patients are also Jewish—one must guard against the facile conclusion that Jews have more emotional problems than other people. This may simply mean that Jews are more willing (and less afraid) to probe the human psyche, to investigate the always fascinating source of emotional turmoil, however painful it may be. One should also bear in mind that among certain groups in our society (writers, painters, actors, professors and people in publishing, advertising, the broadcast media, academia and café society) being psychoanalyzed is often a "social must." Not to have a shrink to talk about at a cocktail party is almost as gauche as not having a tax shelter. Consequently, incest and other sexual aberrations may seem to be more prevalent within this select group of people, when, in fact, it is merely more publicized. And this may account for Dr. Kinsey's skepticism when he referred to "some psychologists who contend that they have never had a patient who has not had incestuous relations." But we still don't know if these psychologists were referring to *actual* incest or *fantasized* incest.

## ACTUAL INCESTUOUS RELATIONSHIPS

As several recent books indicate, incest is not an isolated perversion confined to the sleazy Southern towns of Faulkner and James Dickey; it is virtually epidemic in all levels of society. In her book, *Betrayal of Innocence*, Susan Forward estimates that more than ten million Americans have been involved in incestuous relationships.

Her figures are derived from American Humane Association reports which indicate that one out of every four women is a victim of sexual molestation by the time she reaches the age of eighteen, and that 38 percent of these abuses are incestuous. The concept of daughters as property—as sexual chattel— accounts for the most repeated violations. More than 75 percent of all reported incest cases involve fathers and daughters, with the mother often "an enigmatic figure" in the background, apparently choosing to ignore what is going on. Her inability to maintain a viable relationship with either her husband or daughter may underlie her seeming acquiescence.

One victim told Forward: "We were all starved in my family—not for food, we always had plenty of money—but for feelings. Nobody ever seemed to feel anything. At least when I had sex with my father I could feel something."

Most psychologists agree that incest invariably leads to lifelong emotional scars for the victim, the aggressor and the "silent partner" (generally the mother) who consciously or unconsciously allows the act to take place. The silent partner often pulls back from her family in an attempt to evade her emotional duties, Forward asserts. "Disappointed and bored with her husband, she seeks fulfillment elsewhere, dealing with problems ranging from housekeeping to sex by passing them along to her daughter."

One of my respondents:

"I remember my father tickling me down there between my legs, but it was only when he was sort of drunk. My mother would get awful mad at him, and a couple of times she actually slapped him. That always surprised me when I was a little kid because I thought he was just tickling me for fun."

## SEX BETWEEN ADULTS AND CHILDREN_____

Almost every day, somewhere in the United States, some man is arrested and charged with molesting or attempting to rape a child. Though many of these arrests and subsequent indictments are based on irrefutable evidence, quite a few are the products of a temporary community hysteria caused by a recent child-rape or murder in that particular locale. Several years ago, when Fred Stroble was convicted of a gruesome child murder in a Los Angeles suburb, the surrounding community was so traumatized that the police were inundated with scores of unfounded complaints of child molestation in all sections of the San Fernando Valley. The situation became so exacerbated that affectionate, demonstrative men were suddenly afraid to pat the head of a neighbor's child for fear of being accused of attempted rape. One mail carrier, who had been extremely popular with the children on his route because he occasionally tickled their ribs and clowned with them, was suddenly transferred to office duty because a local woman complained that he was "getting too sexy with my kids."

Unfortunately, there are some men—some of them even elderly—who are dangerously attracted to young children, who may try to engage them in various kinds of sexual activity and who may even murder a child in a moment of irrepressible madness. Some psychologists have described these offenders as "sexually thwarted," incapable of gaining the attention of adult women and thus reduced to frantic attempts to gain the attention of innocent children unable to defend themselves. Years ago Kinsey suggested a more benign view in relation to elderly offenders, calling for "an interpretation which would more nearly fit our understanding of old age—which would recognize the decline in erotic reaction, the loss of capacity to perform, and the reduction of the emotional life of the individual to such affectionate fondling as parents and especially grandparents are wont to bestow upon their own (and other) children." Nevertheless, many small girls reflect the public hysteria over the prospect of "being touched" by a strange person; and many a child who has no idea of the mechanics of intercourse interprets affection and simple caressing, from anyone except her own parents, as attempts at rape. Thus, as one authority put it, "not a few older men serve time in penal institutions for attempting to engage in a sexual act which at their age would not interest most of them, and of which many of them are undoubtedly incapable."

None of the men I interviewed had ever been criminally involved with a child, but five of them freely expressed a preference for young girls—and two of them had had sexual relations with child prostitutes aged thirteen or fourteen. One of these five men told me about "this friend of mine who really goes for young girls. He's a corporate executive who travels a lot to Puerto Rico, where he met this thirteen-year-old prostitute that he fell in love with. He kept seeing her every time he went to San Juan—practically every month. And that lasted for about two years. Then he suddenly decided she was getting too old. Her tits had gotten too full and her body had started to fill out like a grown woman—so he found himself another thirteen-year-old girl. Which I sort of understand, because there's something really appealing in younger girls—like they're still innocent and haven't been around too much."

From the curious expression on his face and his closing comment, I got the immediate impression that he was actually talking about himself.

Another respondent, one of the two who admitted having sex with a child prostitute, expressed a certain amount of guilt about his involvement with a thirteen-year-old girl in Tijuana. "I got to thinking about my own thirteen-year-old daughter, and that made me feel pretty shitty. But I keep looking for young girls. I feel safer with them."

From the limited number of male respondents who admitted having sexual relations with young girls—prostitutes or otherwise—it would be impossible to determine any variations between WASPs, Catholics or Jews. And the same would hold true for older women who engage in sex with young males. But there is one substantial difference: Older women (generally in their thirties or forties) do not seek involvements with thirteen- and fourteen-year-old boys. The few that do have sexual contact with much younger males generally choose boys between sixteen and twenty years of age. Thus, the "dirty old man" syndrome, which usually refers to men past fifty, has no observable parallel among women.

With respect to fantasies of sex with young girls, about 20 percent of the male respondents directly or indirectly admitted having had at least one dream in which they had performed some type of sexual act with a female under fifteen years of age. Only 3 percent of the female interviewees reported fantasies about boys under fifteen, but about 30 percent admitted dreaming about sexual intercourse with boys between sixteen and twenty years of age—usually with youngsters who deliver groceries or mow the lawn. Some of their comments are perhaps more significant than the bare statistics:

"Like I wouldn't never do something like that—not actually—but I've sometimes dreamed about a little sex with some young girl. Now, there's this cute little friend of my daughter—really sort of sexy for someone only thirteen years old—and I've dreamed about having her. But I always make her a little older in my dream—so that ain't so bad."

"Well, I'm not sure I would ever do it, but I've got this friend who's been having sex with this grocery boy—I mean the one who delivers in this neighborhood. But that's really not too bad, because he's pretty mature for sixteen or maybe seventeen. He's really got a good body for his age, and I imagine she's not the only one who's having him. You can tell he's had plenty of experience—like he's got this real sexy manner. Which is the way my husband used to be way back then, when he still had something going . . ."

"There's nothing wrong with having someone younger, as long as it's not some snot-nosed kid. But you take some of these sixteen or seventeen-year-old boys, they're already pretty mature, some of them. And it's sort of fun to teach them new things about sex, which they'd never get from these stupid little cheerleader types."

"Almost any guy can have a dream about sex with some young girl. For example, that picture show where Laurence Olivier gets involved with that little sexpot named Lolita. Well, after I saw that movie, I had three or four dreams about her—and also about this neighborhood girl who came by to sell us some Girl Scout cookies. I bought six boxes, and my wife wondered what the hell was wrong with me. Anyway, I took the damned cookies to the office, and that was that. But I wouldn't ever even touch a kid like that—never. Dreaming is one thing, but actually doing is something else."

It is interesting to note that even those persons who have fantasized about sex with young girls and boys are opposed to *actual* intercourse between adults and children. Indeed, almost 100 percent of my 722 interviewees—including three of the five men who had actually participated in such acts—vehemently condemned such behavior with respect to young girls. But at least 30 percent (mostly women) expressed no qualms about actual intercourse with young boys—assuming, of course, that they were past sixteen.

## ETHNIC VARIATIONS_____

*Here, however, there is an ethnic variation.* Among the gentile respondents, 25 percent would tolerate and/or encourage sexual relations between adult women and older teenage boys; whereas a significantly larger number of Jewish women, about 35 percent of those interviewed, would tolerate or favor such involvements. One should also note that Catholic women seem more accepting than Protestants in this regard. As for the male respondents—many of whom favored sex with girls between the ages of seventeen and twenty—a large majority, close to 75 percent, either opposed or jokingly dismissed the idea of adult women having intercourse with boys of the same age. Nevertheless, Jewish men seemed somewhat more liberal than gentiles in this respect. "I wouldn't necessarily like it if my wife did it," one of them remarked. "But, speaking in the abstract, I guess women are entitled. I myself got initiated by a forty-year-old woman when I mowed her lawn. She paid me five dollars an hour—for the mowing, I mean—and that was thirty years ago, when a dollar an hour was the going rate."

## HOMOSEXUALITY AND LESBIANISM_____

Although still taboo in most levels of society, homosexuality and lesbianism have seemingly become more acceptable during the past decade, certainly in such metropolitan areas as New York, San Francisco and Los Angeles. Expanding beyond the fields of dress design, interior decoration, hair styling, the theater, graphic arts and the broadcast media, where their presence had been fairly visible for many years, homosexuals have increasingly surfaced in publishing houses, college campuses, public schools, social work agencies and various branches of the civil service. (The word "surfaced" is intentional, since they have, in fact, worked in these professions for a long time, carefully concealing their sexual preferences for fear of instant ostracism.) In most places and in most occupations, however, they are still *persona non grata.*

Perhaps because they themselves have been heavily involved in most of these occupations and professions, Jews have apparently accepted homosexuals more readily than gentiles.

As one very successful (and heterosexual) television director once told me, "As a lifetime Jew, I know how it feels to be an outsider. Besides, if I didn't hire them, I'd have a helluva time putting on a show—or it might be a pretty crappy one, 'cause there's an awful lot of homosexual talent in this business—off camera as well as on camera." It is rather difficult to imagine a Wall Street or IBM executive making that kind of statement.

Aside from their acceptance or tolerance of deviant sexual behavior, it would be difficult to ascertain whether gentiles or Jews are more apt to be lesbian or homosexual. On a per capita basis, this survey showed no measurable difference between the two groups.

But with respect to attitudes concerning homosexuality or lesbianism, there were some significant variations. So as to personalize their reactions in specific terms, I asked our respondents the following questions:

(a)  Would you want to work with or hire a homosexual or lesbian?

    60% of gentile women — yes
    30% of gentile women — no
    10% of gentile women — no opinion

    50% of gentile men   — yes
    40% of gentile men   — no
    10% of gentile men   — no opinion

    75% of Jewish women — yes
    20% of Jewish women — no
     5% of Jewish women — no opinion

    70% of Jewish men    — yes
    25% of Jewish men    — no
     5% of Jewish men    — no opinion

(b)  Would you socialize with a homosexual or lesbian?

    40% of gentile women — yes
    50% of gentile women — no
    10% of gentile women — no opinion

    35% of gentile men   — yes
    60% of gentile men   — no
     5% of gentile men   — no opinion

    60% of Jewish women — yes

35% of Jewish women — no
5% of Jewish women — no opinion
50% of Jewish men   — yes
40% of Jewish men   — no
10% of Jewish men   — no opinion

As one might expect, some of their individual comments reveal a far wider range of attitude than a simple Yes or No:

"I don't have anything against queers, mind you—but I sure don't want any of them coming around my house. Like I've got my kids to think about, and how they might get influenced by one of these people."

"Well, my husband wouldn't want us to socialize with any homosexuals, but he's got hang-ups about all kinds of people. Now, I personally wouldn't mind. In fact, most of them would be a lot more fun at a party than my husband's dull friends. All they can talk about is football or baseball or about how drunk they got at some party. I'd much rather talk with someone like my hairdresser. Now, he's got a real sense of humor and can talk about all sorts of interesting things."

"Our best friend is a homosexual, and he's about the most decent man I know."

"Listen, if a guy wants to be queer, he should stick to his own kind. I sure don't want them around me. They really give you the creeps—I mean that sissy way they talk and everything else."

"My brother's a homosexual, and I frankly don't care what he is. Like he's always been my best friend—someone I could always trust. But I know my husband is uncomfortable with him, so I seldom invite Bill to our parties, which really gripes me when I stop to think about it. Anyway, Bill and I have lunch about once a week, and he sort of jokes about my square husband."

"Lesbians are a lot easier to socialize with, especially if they're not openly butch. My best friend is a lesbian, but very few people are aware of it. Most of our friends just think of her as a very independent career woman who hasn't got time for men."

"About a year ago one of the women in our consciousness-raising group suddenly decided to leave her husband and two kids and moved into a lesbian commune. Most of our social group turned against her—shut her out completely. Except for me. But when I asked her to stay for dinner one night (after she had dropped in for an afternoon visit), my husband suddenly announced that he had to go back to his office. He didn't even try to be polite or subtle about it. Then the very next day he actually ordered me not to see Dorrie anymore. So I told him to go to hell, and I still invite her over whenever I damn well please."

"If it weren't for our homosexual friends, our parties would be dull as hell."

"I'm gay and I'm proud of it. But I used to pretend to be straight so as not to embarrass my friends out in Scarsdale. I'd always go to their parties with a date—usually one of the models for our agency. I imagine some of those suburban Joes assumed I was a big cocksman, but most of their wives probably knew better. Women are harder to fool on that score. Anyway, I finally decided to cut out the bullshit pretence, and I showed up with my real lover, which pissed off most of the men, but some of the women weren't the least bit annoyed. In fact, three of them—including the hostess—seemed to approve what I'd done. But I haven't been to Scarsdale for a long time—almost a year now."

"I'm the token gay and the token black. So I'm naturally invited to more parties than I can possibly attend."

"One of my wife's friends is a homosexual, which is okay by me. But, quite frankly, I'd rather not invite him to certain parties where we're entertaining some of my squarer clients. Yet I would never dare tell Lucy not to invite him. She'd cut off my balls . . . or worse—if there *is* anything worse."

"My husband and I are in the theater business, so we've always had a few homosexual friends. But when we realized that our oldest son was homosexual, it was a pretty shaky experience at first. He had suppressed himself until he got to college, and then suddenly told us about it in his junior year. I guess we should have seen the signs long before but didn't want to face them. Anyway, we've fully accepted his situation and we've welcomed his male companion to our home and to many of our parties. But once in a while I've noticed my husband momentarily staring at Paul with this puzzled hurt expression in his eyes—and I imagine he's seen the same look in my eyes."

## CELIBACY OR NO-PARTNER SEX

There are some people who have found that sex with another person (whether homosexual or heterosexual) is unsatisfactory or too much of an emotional strain, thus opting for either celibacy or autoeroticism. One such person, Ziva Kwitney, associate editor of *Catalog of Sexual Consciousness,* described her ambivalence as follows:

*There were times when the passion was not intense enough to sustain me through a half hour of lovemaking. (Sometimes, in the middle of the sex act, I would have a fantasy of rising from the bed like an apparition, to hover in midair above my partner and ask him, sweetly, would he mind finishing without me.) I was, however, raised to be polite; and I trained myself to be realistic: did I expect to wait forever for the perfect lover while my loins ached and my prime passed inexorably by?*

*Sex, I discovered, was not simple—at least not for me. I expended too much energy tending to my displaced emotions (or his) and what I got out of it simply wasn't satisfying enough, either to my soul or to my cunt . . .*

*Thereafter, I decided, despite occasional bursts of lust, to forgo sex with partners. I did not deny myself light or casual physical contact with men or women—I simply avoided genital contact. I purchased a vibrator. I found sensual gratification in massage with women and men I cared for. I decided to trust myself to know when to attempt a union again . . .*

I have no data with respect to ethnic differences in this type of autoeroticism, but I rather suspect that it is probably related more to social class than to culture, that it is less prevalent among lower-class females than among middle- or upper-class women.

# 9
# Marriage & Other Life-Styles

EXTRAMARITAL SEX —————————————————————

Although the institution of marriage has been steadily weakened during the past two decades, most Americans still prefer some type of legal and/or religious sanction when they decide to live together—even though almost 50 percent of them will be divorced at some future date. Needless to say, many people stay married despite acute unhappiness with their spouses, because they cannot or simply do not wish to cope with the trauma of divorce, the prospective misery of loneliness apparently seeming more intolerable than the continuing misery of a bad marriage. Consequently, extramarital sex would seem to offer at least a temporary escape from a loveless relationship—but, as one New York psychologist recently remarked, "Screwing someone else doesn't necessarily mean that you're unhappily married."

In any event, extramarital sex has been increasing in all parts of the country—urban, suburban and rural—and in all levels of society, and the tide of promiscuity seems endless. Indeed, there are very few people who do not know someone who has "cheated" on his or her spouse, themselves included. However, given the surreptitious nature of such behavior, there is no way of ascertaining with any statistical accuracy how many married persons do in fact engage in extramarital fornication. And, *ipso facto*, there is no way of determining whether Catholics and Protestants are more promiscuous than Jews, or vice versa. Nevertheless, it was possible to ascertain how a certain representative sample of the population reacts to such behavior, as set forth in answers to the questions cited below. Quite obviously, many of the respondents would probably have

answered differently if they had been asked the same question
in the presence of their spouses or at an open public meeting.

Q: How do you feel about extramarital sex? Do you strongly
disapprove, moderately disapprove, slightly disapprove,
highly approve, moderately approve or minimally approve?

*Protestant females*

| | |
|---|---|
| Strongly disapprove | 15% |
| Moderately disapprove | 25% |
| Slightly disapprove | 15% |
| Highly approve | 5% |
| Moderately approve | 25% |
| Minimally approve | 15% |

*Protestant males*

| | |
|---|---|
| Strongly disapprove | 15% |
| Moderately disapprove | 15% |
| Slightly disapprove | 10% |
| Highly approve | 15% |
| Moderately approve | 25% |
| Minimally approve | 20% |

*Catholic females*

| | |
|---|---|
| Strongly disapprove | 20% |
| Moderately disapprove | 25% |
| Slightly disapprove | 15% |
| Highly approve | 5% |
| Moderately approve | 25% |
| Minimally approve | 10% |

*Catholic males*

| | |
|---|---|
| Strongly disapprove | 15% |
| Moderately disapprove | 15% |
| Slightly disapprove | 5% |
| Highly approve | 10% |
| Moderately approve | 30% |
| Minimally approve | 25% |

*Jewish females*

| | |
|---|---|
| Strongly disapprove | 10% |
| Moderately disapprove | 20% |
| Slightly disapprove | 10% |
| Highly approve | 10% |

| Moderately approve | 30% |
| Slightly approve | 20% |

*Jewish males*

| Strongly disapprove | 10% |
| Moderately disapprove | 15% |
| Slightly disapprove | 5% |
| Highly approve | 15% |
| Moderately approve | 30% |
| Minimally approve | 25% |

*Q:* Would you ask for a divorce if you should find out that your wife/husband has engaged in sexual relations with another person?

*Protestant females*

| Yes | 30% |
| Probably | 40% |
| No | 30% |

*Protestant males*

| Yes | 50% |
| Probably | 35% |
| No | 15% |

*Catholic females*

| Yes | 30% |
| Probably | 10% |
| No | 60% |

*Catholic males*

| Yes | 45% |
| Probably | 30% |
| No | 25% |

*Jewish females*

| Yes | 15% |
| Probably | 15% |
| No | 70% |

*Jewish males*

| Yes | 35% |
| Probably | 20% |
| No | 45% |

While asking the first of these two questions, I got the distinct impression that most of the women were imagining their husbands engaging in extramarital affairs, while most of the men were thinking about themselves having sex with other women. This seems to be borne out by the males' seemingly contradictory answers to the second question, in which the macho double standard is revealed in a glaring light. In other words, 60 to 70 percent of the male interviewees approved (in varying degrees) of extramarital sex *in the abstract*—but 75 to 85 percent of the gentile males would consider divorce if their wives were to get sexually involved with someone else. With respect to the Jewish respondents, 60 percent of the females and 70 percent of the males approved (in varying degrees) of extramarital sex—but, here again, the male double standard surfaced when both sexes were asked if they would consider filing for divorce if they should ever discover that their spouse had committed adultery: 55 percent of the men said "yes" or "probably," while only 30 percent of the women would be so inclined.

Judging from their facial expressions and their voice quality—as well as from my own experience as a lawyer—I strongly suspect that many of these women meant "probably not" when they said "probably," whereas most of the men were less ambivalent about that word. But aside from such semantic speculation, it is interesting to note the decidedly liberal attitude of Jewish women on both questions. Only 40 percent expressed varying degrees of disapproval regarding extramarital sex, as compared with 55 percent for Protestant women and 60 percent for Catholic women. As for filing for divorce on the grounds of adultery, only 30 percent of female Jewish respondents said "yes" or "probably"—as compared with 70 percent for Protestant women and 40 percent for Catholic women. (One should note that this latter percentage probably reflects a religious objection to divorce rather than a willingness to accept a husband's transgression.) Jewish men are similarly more liberal than Protestants or Catholics on both issues, but to a lesser degree.

To add a substance to the bare statistics, I offer herewith a random selection of comments that are difficult to categorize for statistical purposes:

"Look, when a man fools around with some other dame, that's a lot different than when your own wife screws another guy. With a man a little outside nooky don't mean anything—but a woman gets her emotions involved, and that's really violating your marriage."

"Naturally, I wouldn't like it if I should find out my husband is laying another woman (which I sort of suspect anyway), but I wouldn't divorce him just because of that. As my mother always says, 'It's not a perfect world.' So maybe I'd confront him with the evidence and make him promise to lay off—or, better yet, I'll do a little cheating myself. Lovers aren't that hard to find."

"Since I'm a Catholic, I don't think I would divorce him, and I don't know what I'd do. Maybe I wouldn't let him touch me for a while. Make him sleep on the couch—like he's on probation or something. Or maybe I'd make him talk to our parish priest."

"Maybe I'd kill her—or at least beat the hell out of her. No woman is gonna put horns on me and get away with it. And not only would I divorce her, I would damn well take the kids from her. There are plenty of women who could take her place and be good mothers to them. I got two right now who wouldn't mind marrying me, and they're both a lot better in bed than she is. So why should I take any crap?"

"I don't know if my wife has ever had any affairs with other men—but if she has, she has certainly been discreet. And that's about all you can hope for: discretion. People who openly flaunt their affairs are merely engaging in vengeance fucking; and when someone gets to that stage, he or she ought to get a divorce and have done with it."

"I guess I would shut my eyes and close my ears and not let myself know about it. It's not that I love him that much—which sometimes I don't—but I doubt that my pride could stand that kind of thing. So if he ever does fool around, I hope no one tells me."

"Myself, I figure women are like men—they need a little variety now and then. So long as she's careful and quiet about it, how would I really know? But, frankly, I wouldn't like it to happen like it does with my friend Saul, whose wife screws around in technicolor . . . and on a wide screen yet. They should call it screw-orama."

"Listen, you're asking a question that's already past history. I caught my husband shacking up in a fancy motel with this floozy buyer from his own shop. So I raised hell for a couple of weeks, but I wasn't about to divorce him and give him that satisfaction, 'cause maybe that's what he was really looking for. Better yet, I decided to look for someone myself—younger maybe. Like the saying goes, there's plenty of goose for any gander that wants it."

"Nothing would hurt me more, I mean really. But I wouldn't know how to react, because I've done a little screwing around myself—like any other guy. Anyway, I don't really want to think about my wife having an affair. It's not the kind of question I can honestly answer."

"I would want to divorce him—if I could get up the courage to face the loneliness. But, you know, there are some things far worse than adultery. For example, there's that mean, awful way that men put down a woman and makes her feel like dirt, that takes away any shred of dignity, that's the worst part—what he does to you in your own house, not what he does to some stupid chippy in a cheap motel."

"To tell you the truth, I've had a suspicion that my wife has had a lover for a long time. With this guy she knew in high school, who's now some kind of big shot at IBM. But I don't have any real proof—just little things that kind of raise your suspicion, and keep you awake thinking and thinking while she's sleeping like some innocent kid. I look at that smile that comes on her face, as if she's dreaming about being with him, and I want to wake her up all of a sudden and try to catch her saying his name. But I never do. I just lie there, letting my gut go sour, til I finally doze off."

## WIFE OR HUSBAND SWAPPING

There are, of course, certain couples who have mutually agreed to "open marriages," wherein both spouses are free to have sexual relations with outside lovers. Some seek to preserve a certain marital coziness by inviting another couple to join them for an evening of friendly copulation, a jolly foursome with less complications than bridge. The more gregarious swingers prefer larger enclaves, sometimes referred to as orgies, where the choice of surrogate spouses is more varied and numerous, a sort of erotic smorgasbord with unlimited seconds.

In recent years spouse-swapping has become institutionalized, with an increasing network of apparently insatiable lovers communicating through newsletters or ads in underground newspapers or straight trade journals, some of which may be innocently publishing discreet come-ons that somehow escape close editorial scrutiny. Ultimately, as one might expect in a nation committed to commercial get-up-and-go, several astute entrepreneurs organized clubs in lovely secluded areas for the benefit of swingers who might feel some discomfort exchanging bed partners in their own homes, where an inquisitive child might occasionally wonder why mommy had shut herself in the bedroom with Mr. Woolsy. Among the most celebrated clubs is Sandstone, which is located in the lovely environs of Topanga Canyon, not far from the ocean-front mansions of the famous Malibu Colony in Southern California.

One would expect to find a host of freewheeling liberated bohemians at Sandstone, but one journalistic visitor was surprised to learn that most of the nude spouse-swappers were "kind of square and conservative about everything except sex." And even in this respect, most of them addressed themselves to the task of copulation with a joyless, mechanical concentration that reminded one of robots in heat. Having observed them solemnly exchanging one naked partner for another, the reporter was not at all surprised to learn that almost all of them (car salesmen, druggists, insurance brokers, bakery owners, minor business executives, computer program specialists) had voted for Richard Nixon and opposed busing and the Equal Rights Amendment.

Although there has been some research on spouse-swapping, there is no way of reaching an accurate estimate of the number of couples who are involved in open or covert exchanges. Only two (less than one-third of 1 percent) of my interviewees admitted having swapped spouses, and one of them told me that her former husband had divorced her because she was the one who had initially suggested exchanging mates with a couple they had met while camping in Colorado. "I really thought my husband wanted to—he certainly seemed to enjoy it—but several months later he told me that he had just gone along because he didn't want to look like a square. So that's when he asked for a divorce."

Although most of the respondents disapproved of spouse-swapping, the women seemed slightly less opposed than the men. Below is a breakdown of their reactions to the following question:

Q:How do you feel about married couples openly agreeing to have sexual relations with other partners? Do you approve, disapprove or feel indifferent?

*Protestant females*

| | |
|---|---|
| Approve | None |
| Disapprove | 90% |
| Indifferent | 10% |

*Catholic females*

| | |
|---|---|
| Approve | .03% |
| Disapprove | 90% |
| Indifferent | 9.07% |

*Jewish females*

| | |
|---|---|
| Approve | None |
| Disapprove | 85% |
| Indifferent | 15% |

*Protestant males*

| | |
|---|---|
| Approve | None |
| Disapprove | 95% |
| Indifferent | 5% |

*Catholic males*

| | |
|---|---|
| Approve | .03% |
| Disapprove | 95% |
| Indifferent | 4.07% |

*Jewish males*

| | |
|---|---|
| Approve | None |
| Disapprove | 90% |
| Indifferent | 10% |

Here are some comments from respondents:

"You have to be a real pervert to let your wife screw some other guy, even though you might want to screw his wife. But switching around ain't for me, not by a long shot."

"Well, I've sometimes dreamed about swapping husbands with one of my friends, who's married to a sexy guy. But I'd never think of actually doing it. And I know my husband would never agree to it."

"My wife and I met this swinging couple in Miami, and they sort of hinted that we ought to get together for a little switch-around. Well, they made it sound sort of tempting, and my wife seemed vaguely interested, but we decided not to get involved."

"I can't think of anything sicker or more perverted than swapping wives and husbands. How could you possibly face your priest—or even your own self—after doing something that filthy?"

"I've heard of people doing that sort of thing, but they must be real creeps. How could you possibly allow your own wife to sleep with some other man?"

"Married couples who do that sort of thing haven't got much of a marriage."

"It makes me sick to hear that people would actually switch their very own husbands and wives that way. To me that's not really sex—it's just perversion."

## THE GET-EVEN CLUB

During the final phase of my sex survey I met two women who were engaged in a novel experiment that could be considered a female equivalent of the macho syndrome. Having participated for many months in weekly group therapy sessions conducted by a neo-Freudian analyst, Shari Ryan and Joan Davis (as I shall call them) had become intimate friends from their very first meeting, their friendship having been strengthened by the mutual knowledge that their respective husbands were chronic womanizers.

During one of their Wednesday-evening sessions Joan had told the group about her husband's constant philandering since less than a year after their marriage. "He's had at least one new woman every month," she said. "And all of them are gentiles—every one of them. He's been keeping a diary about his affairs in a red datebook, which I found in his office desk one afternoon. But some day I'll get even with him. I'm going to seduce a different man every month. I'll call it "The Get-Even Club." She had smiled when she said it, but there were tears in her eyes.

Later that evening Joan and Shari had continued the discussion at a nearby bar. "I like your idea," said Shari. "And if you're really serious, I'll join the club. We can exchange lovers and compare notes on them. But this Catholic lady likes Jewish lovers. I met two of them when I was at Vassar, and they were great. As a matter of fact, I still can't explain why I went and married another mick like me."

"Ethnic bias," said Joan. "I did the same thing—married

my own kind, as my mother used to say. But it's time for a change, at least for me."

Thus, Joan's joking threat became a reality. Within five days they got their first man, a smooth-talking WASP who worked in a big advertising agency on Madison Avenue. Joan had met him in Bloomingdale's fancy food section, near the cheese counter, where she coyly allowed herself to be picked up. The very next day she passed him over to Shari, and they celebrated their first "score" at a midtown restaurant.

"That was a real joyride," said Joan, sipping a champagne cocktail. "But he's got the cheesiest line I've ever heard."

"That's a cute name for it," said Shari. "Let's call them joyrides from now on. That will be our code for anyone we screw."

It was Shari who told me about the southern Baptist who always ate peanuts after intercourse, carefully shelling them with an expert snap of his fingers. "He'd put the damned shells in one of his shoes and would later empty them into the john. He claimed that 'peanuts replace all the protein lost in ejaculated semen,' and those were his exact words!" This particular man was a high school chemistry teacher from Montgomery, Alabama, whom Shari had met while he was feeding the monkeys at the Central Park Zoo. His sharp angular features, curiously contrasted with his soft deep-South drawl, had instantly attracted her, though she was later dismayed by the solemn mechanical way in which he made love. Joan was equally dismayed by his sexual performance but was nonetheless fascinated and amused by his peanut act and his dead-serious explanation about replenishing his protein supply. He apparently repeated the same phrase, word for word, as if he were dictating a chemical formula to a group of high school students.

As one might expect, the two club members were most apt to focus their memories on the lovers who exhibited some odd quirk rather than those who were merely competent or extremely virile. The man they remembered most readily was "the hummer," a rather baldish Italian man whom Shari had met at a well-known Italian restaurant. Although they did not consider him an expert or exciting lover, they were impressed by his endurance. He was always able to have intercourse for at least an hour without reaching climax, and while doing so, he always hummed a tune, the same tune, over and over again, as if he were a broken record. But for each woman he hummed a different tune. For Shari it was Ravel's "Bolero," and for Joan he hummed "Moon Over Miami," always adjusting his own bodily rhythm to whatever song he had chosen.

"Do you always hum when you're having sex?" Shari had asked him.

"Only when I'm having sex or dressing a corpse," he said quite matter-of-factly.

"Oh, my god, don't tell me you're a coroner!"

"No, nothing like that," he said. "I'm just an ordinary mortician. Have my own shop in Omaha. That's in Nebraska, you know. Near McCook."

"Well, what do you hum to your corpses?" she asked. "Some kind of religious tunes?"

"Not at all, honey. I just hum the same kind of songs I hum to live people—when I'm making love, I mean. That way I don't get too emotionally involved in what I'm doing."

Joan later tried to get her husband (who would always come to climax in less than thirty seconds) to extend his performance by humming "Moon Over Miami." But he rejected her suggestion instantly, a shade of suspicion in his sudden anger. "Jesus, you're getting freaky as hell. Where're you getting all these weird ideas? I mean you're really something, baby. I can't tell where you're coming from when you get on this sex kick."

## UNMARRIED COUPLES

Although there have always been certain couples living together without benefit of marriage, there has been a sharp increase in such arrangements during the past few years, particularly among middle-class college students. Indeed, in some social circles unmarried couples are as common as macrobiotic diets.

This trend is easily detected on college campuses in the Northeast and on the West Coast, with fewer numbers in the usually more conservative areas of the South and Midwest. In fact, certain universities have openly tolerated such unions, so that male and female students share quarters in coed college dorms. "Like it's no big deal to shack with your old lady," remarked a slender freshman, dangling his bony arm around the shoulders of his seventeen-year-old "old lady." Whether or not their parents are similarly unimpressed is a different question. Our survey indicates that mothers are more tolerant about such arrangements than fathers are, especially when it's a daughter involved. As one Madison Avenue executive confided to his analyst, "I wouldn't mind my son shacking with some coed, but I sure don't feel right about my daughter living with someone. After all, she's only a kid, and she could get pregnant."

As the following statistical breakdown clearly shows, attitudes toward unmarried cohabitation do vary according to ethnic background:

Q: Do you approve or disapprove of young people living together without being married?

*Protestant females*

| | |
|---|---|
| Approve | 30% |
| Disapprove | 60% |
| Indifferent | 10% |

*Catholic females*

| | |
|---|---|
| Approve | 20% |
| Disapprove | 70% |
| Indifferent | 10% |

*Jewish females*

| | |
|---|---|
| Approve | 40% |
| Disapprove | 40% |
| Indifferent | 20% |

*Protestant males*

| | |
|---|---|
| Approve | 20% |
| Disapprove | 75% |
| Indifferent | 5% |

*Catholic males*

| | |
|---|---|
| Approve | 15% |
| Disapprove | 75% |
| Indifferent | 10% |

*Jewish males*

| | |
|---|---|
| Approve | 35% |
| Disapprove | 50% |
| Indifferent | 15% |

"It makes no difference what you think. If your daughter wants to live with some student, she's going to do it no matter what you say. That's the kind of world we're living in these days. No respect for anything."

"What could be more natural than two people living together at any age? I only wish I had been able to do the same thing. Maybe if I'd lived for a while with my husband, I wouldn't have married him. This way you have a chance to really know someone before you make it permanent. So I want my daughter to try it first—even though my husband thinks I'm a loose woman when I say it."

"How can any man want his own daughter to shack up with some kid who's still in school? It's not only immoral, it's stupid. That's why we've got so goddamned many illegitimate kids running around. Some young kid gets your daughter pregnant and takes off for Mexico, where he'll find someone else to live with."

"Look, I wouldn't mind my son living with his girl friend, 'cause that might give him a little experience—not only the sex part, but also getting to know what a crock of shit marriage is going to be."

"Kids these days don't know what they're getting into. They don't look at the future—especially these young girls, like my own daughter maybe—so they can't realize that no guy wants to marry someone who's had a kid without getting married. Right away people get the idea she was just sleeping around."

"My husband's uptight about our daughter living with her boyfriend in a college dorm; and, quite frankly, I'm not too happy about it. But I'm sure it will give her some insight into marriage and what it's like to live with a man."

"All I'm hoping for is that he doesn't get her pregnant. Jerry isn't ready to be a father. He's got to finish college first."

# 10
# Women's Lib &
# New Sex

*So do men look to destroy every quality in a woman which will give
her the powers of a male, for she is in their eyes already armed with
the power that she brought them forth, and that is a power beyond
measure—the earliest etchings of memory go back to that woman
between whose legs they were conceived, nurtured, and near-
strangled in the hours of birth . . .*

—Norman Mailer, *The Prisoner of Sex*

## THE MALE-FEMALE
## STRUGGLE FOR PRIMACY

The male-female struggle for sexual primacy is as old as the
very beginnings of human existence. On the walls of the most
ancient cave dwellings, archeologists have found crude carvings
that offer unmistakable evidence of male chauvinism and apparent female submission; but as women later acquired the
means of expressing their real feelings, their profound resentment of male dominance, the struggle became, if not more
equal, certainly more interesting. Indeed, as we come into the
final quarter of the twentieth century, there is reason to hope
that women will finally achieve sexual equality and perhaps (to
use an Orwellian phrase) will become "more equal" than men.
In any event, some notable male-female encounters are taking
place on the battlefield of literature, and the most bitterly fierce
contenders are male and female writers who have entered the
fray with the keenly honed intellectual weaponry of their common Jewish heritage.

Some observers feel that the Women's Liberation Movement has been the principal cause of this now-open conflict, but
we are inclined to agree with those who consider Women's Lib-

eration a mere symptom of an age-old syndrome, a long-simmering fever that has finally burst into a furious boil. And what is more likely to keep that fever at a high boil than the following excerpts from the work of three of the most successful Jewish novelists:

*History had decreed that men and women had to become acquainted in these embraces. I was going to find out whether or not Renata was my Fate, or whether the true Jungian anima was in her. She might turn out to be something far different. But one sexual touch would teach me that, for women had peculiar effects on me, and if they didn't make me ecstatic they made me ill. There were no two ways about it.*

—Saul Bellow, *Humboldt's Gift*

*Till Maureen I had never even fought a man in anger—with my hands, that is; but I was much more combative at 25 than I am now and learned quickly enough how to disarm her of her favorite weapon, the spike of a high-heeled shoe. Eventually I came to realize that not even a good shaking such as parents administer to recalcitrant children was sufficient to stop her once she was on the warpath—it required a slap in the face to do that. "Just like Mezik!" screamed Maureen, dropping dramatically to the floor to cower before my violence (and pretending as best as she could that it did not give her pleasure to have uncovered the brute in the high-minded young artist).*

—Philip Roth, *My Life as a Man*

*Miller captured something in the sexuality of men as it had never been seen before, precisely that it was man's sense of awe before woman, his dread of her position one step closer to eternity (for in that step were her powers) which made men detest women, revile them, humiliate them, defecate symbolically upon them, do everything to reduce them so that one might dare to enter them and take pleasure of them. . . . And it is his genius to show that this (female) power is ready to survive any context or abuse.*

—Norman Mailer, *Genius and Lust: A Journey Through the Major Writings of Henry Miller*

In his lifelong search for masculine experience, including an intense interest in boxing and bullfighting (on both of which he has written with considerable technical expertise and a unique psychic awareness), Mailer has been obsessively concerned with the physical aspects of sex, often comparing intercourse with some aspect of fighting. For example, when his protagonist in *An American Dream* has seduced a German maid, he refers to it as "a bitch of a brawl." Consequently, one would expect him to give high marks to the following passage from Miller's *Sexus*:

*"Go on, give it to me, go on, give it, go on, Oh God, give it, give it to me!" She went from one orgasm to another, pushing, thrusting, raising herself, rolling her ass, lifting her legs and twining them around my neck, groaning, grunting, squealing like a pig, and then suddenly thoroughly exhausted, begging me to finish her off, begging me to shoot. "Shoot it, shoot it . . . I'll go mad." Lying there like a sack of oats, panting, sweating, utterly helpless, utterly played out that she was. I slowly and deliberately rammed my cock back and forth, and when I had enjoyed the chopped sirloin, the mashed potatoes, the gravy and all the spices, I shot my wad into the mouth of her womb that jolted her like an electric charge.*

Anyone who has spent time in the army will have heard somewhat similar and often more colorful and exaggerated boasts of sexual domination, almost inevitably followed by a series of escalated boasts that would have made even Miller blush with erotic inadequacy. In retrospect, one wonders how many faked orgasms were required to erect such towers of macho pride. And, after reading the Hite Report, one may further speculate on the number of women who had to masturbate for genuine orgasms after Miller has left their beds or rolled over for a long night of self-satisfied slumber. But whether in fact or fantasy, Miller and Mailer go on brawling in the bedroom like cunt-drunk boxers blearily determined to go the distance, heart-rendingly afraid that they won't be standing on their feet when the final gong is sounded.

In a brilliantly written and well-reasoned essay on the misogyny of Mailer, Bellow, Roth and Miller for the *Village Voice* in December 1976, Vivian Gornick had this comment on Mailer's premise that men must humiliate women to overcome their awe of her ability to bear children:

*That, says Mailer in all of his books, is at the heart of what passes between human beings who are men and women. The human being who is a man can encounter the human being who is a woman in one way only: he must mount her, fuck her, suck her, penetrate and impale her, conquer and reduce her, for she is not simply another human being like himself but the embodiment of the mysterious heart—the universal elemental source—and it is only through that raging lust, in the Cosmic Fuck, that he can hope to close with the Mysteries of the Inner Space, thus reducing her powers and increasing his own.* That, *says Mailer, is the truth about men and women, and all the rest is totalitarian bullshit. And don't you ever forget it, you Shock Troops of the Liberation, you pathetic dumb-cunt broads (uh, excuse me, you Great Female Power of the Universe). . . . It is now abundantly clear that Mailer will probably go on speaking this sorrowful male-female nonsense, with no more wisdom than he had 25 years ago, until he is in his doddering seventies.*

With respect to Philip Roth, whose earlier stories about Jewish adolescence moved her deeply, Ms. Gornick persuasively suggests that he had lately succumbed to the panic of immature vanity, a preoccupation with self-worth that has made him fatally unaware of the world outside himself. She asks:

*. . . what is the chief element of this obsessive, eaten-up-alive exercise in self-absorption? The hatred of women. With each book the hatred of women looms larger, more nakedly, more desperately in possession of the writer. With each book one sees the horror of a writer who has failed to mature personally, has contrived unsuccessfully to make of that failure a modern myth, and recedes yearly into literary self-delusion.* Portnoy's Complaint *was startling but* My Life as a Man *is frightening. . . . In* My Life as a Man *the wife is monstrous because Roth is saying women are monstrous. When the wife is being beaten to death and surrenders to the ecstasy of what is happening to her, losing control of language as though of her bladder, screaming "Die me, die me!" Roth is clearly saying this repellent creature—and all those who resemble her—deserves to die.*

In Gornick's eyes (and one must note that she perceives the human psyche with an unsettling X-ray clarity), Saul Bellow is no less a misogynist than either Mailer or Roth. Acknowledging the Nobel laureate's undoubted literary brilliance and erudition, she nonetheless feels that his vision has been grossly distorted by his hatred of women. Alluding to the attitudes of Charlie Citrine, "a thinly disguised" Bellow, who is the protagonist of *Humboldt's Gift*, she minces no words as she focuses on "the bilious quality" of the novel, particularly as it relates to women:

*To begin with, the women are uniformly referred to as cunts, broads, chicks, and bimbos. They are all either beautiful or "gorgeous." Then, they are all either thin, cold, intelligent and castrating (these are always the wife) or they are dark, sensual, and mindless (these are the mistress). These characters are like papier-mâché grotesqueries: figures with little magnets affixed to the back of them triggering fantasies of hunger and deprivation. The wife figure flashes: Touch me. I will evoke for you everything in life that is perpetually doing you in. The mistress figure flashes: Touch me. I will evoke for you everything that is perpetually holding out on you.*

With a certain sadness and no little regret, Gornick finally concludes that each of these gifted writers suffers from an infantile self-absorption, and that their fear and hatred of women inevitably warps their perception of humankind, more than half of which is female.

*For me, much of the current work of Mailer, Roth and Bellow is merely therapy, and at that, the worst, the most childish kind of therapy: not the kind that gets to the bottom of things but rather the kind that hardens its defenses, ritualizes human sacrifice, makes do with a primitive kind of bargaining about who's human and who's not. In the misogyny of these writers lies the deluded ancient dream of frightened men: if she is made less human, I will be made more human.*

Gornick is only one of several extremely sensitive women whose writing often reflects the ironic, penetrating humor of their Jewish heritage. There is no whimpering in their novels, short stories and nonfictional work, no frantic appeal for masculine pity. There is, needless to say, much anger and resentment in what they have to say, some of which finds release through what one *Ms.* critic called "a devastating she-wit," and the frequent target of that wit is the Jewish prince—whom many of them know inside out. One example that comes to mind is the spoiled lover in Rhoda Lehrman's *The Girl That He Marries*, a narcissistic would-be politician whose every foible and flaw is dissected with a wicked glee sparked by an impish though penetrating intelligence that will cause some of us male readers to squirm in uneasy recognition of our own macho pretenses. As one reads Lehrman's amused portrayals of several male characters, inevitably identifying with some aspect of each of them, one wonders how long even a Miller-Mailer penis could remain erect in the face of such mocking wit.

The same could be said of Erica Jong's more celebrated *Fear of Flying*, which an anguished male critic defined as "a literary castration." Others, no doubt intending a compliment, likened Jong's freewheeling Rabelaisian humor to Henry Miller's earlier work, failing to note that she is more subtle and sophisticated than Miller, and certainly less self-absorbed and infantile. Where Miller is dead earnest in his *braggadocio*, often sounding like a frightened locker-room jock sensing impending failure in his loins, Jong displays a whimsical detachment that springs from the sexual security of a woman who knows that sex is something more than a pitched battle between opposing egos—that, contrary to the Mailer ethic, no one has to win. Consequently, one can relax and be vastly entertained by the Jongian heroine's merry pursuit of the "zipless fuck," comfortably confident that the author is detached enough to see all the comic possibilities of sex. One revels in the absence of that haunting fear of penis failure that pervades most of the erotic passages penned by Mailer, Roth and Bellow, where much of the potential humor is poisoned by undisguised hate and a frantic need for male dominance, once again stressing the dubious notion that men and women are natural enemies. There are, to be sure, certain portions of *Fear of Flying* in which Jong seems to accept the same premise, but her innate whimsy somehow prevails and enables her to deal with male-female encounters without recourse to hatred or bitterness.

Although men are frequently the targets of their lethal wit, many of the newly successful female novelists often satirize their own sex, using men as mere props for the sadomasochism of the principal character. Thus, in Lois Gould's *Final Analysis*, a psychoanalyzed woman has been shunted off to her Jewish lover's summer house, where she muses about him in the following vein: "He is my ideal lover. He gives me what I really want ... not for him to screw me, but for him to let me screw myself ... So that's what I really love most: hating me. The man who helps me do it is the only lover I understand."

Further exploring the outer limits of masochism in *Such Good Friends*, Gould unravels an excruciatingly painful account of Julie Messinger's raging emotions when she discovers a coded diary of her husband's chronic infidelities, her frustration unbearably exacerbated by the fact that she discovers the damning evidence as he lies comatose in the final throes of death, beyond the reach of any possible vengeance. Remembering how often he had refused her most poignant pleas for affection, she reviews each entry in the diary with a choking fury—positions enjoyed, the number and types of orgasms, the initials of each female conquest, specific dates and coded references to motels and hideaway apartments. Gould spares no feelings as she describes her protagonist's lifelong addiction to man-caused pain, and one is almost tempted to say "enough" when she has Julie fantasize a vengeance fuck with another man while her husband's phantom voice chides the lover for trying to please her: "You can't keep rubbing her goddamn tits all night. I know she likes it . . . You kidding, it's the *only* thing she likes, but whose party *is* this? . . . Can't you just get in and fuck her? . . . You wanna make *her* come?"

In her most recent novel, Lois Gould offers a fascinating symbolic alternative to female vulnerability. In the opening section of *A Sea-Change* the heroine is the helpless victim of a black thug robbing her house, and at the end she is transformed into a black rapist who ravages her best friend. In a wide-ranging critique of female protest fiction for *Ms.* magazine, Josephine Hendin has high praise for Gould's daring use of the transsexual "as a symbol of our deepest ambivalence over vulnerability and power." She goes on to say:

*Gould throws a light on the attempts of every woman who, after a lifetime as a lamb, decides to become a lion. Jessie as the beautiful, passive victim and as the ghetto rapist embodies the yin and yang of sexual anger. Gould uses our old ideas of sex to show our ambivalence about them, to expose our terror of being victims and our fear that in becoming aggressors we will also uncover what is cruel and grotesque in ourselves.*

Hendin has no comment on the implicit racism in Gould's use of a black thug and a black rapist as symbols of ultimate evil, which may simply mean that Ms. Hendin's ardent feminism has no room for such extraneous matters.

There are many other extremely articulate female writers whose work is infused with certain elements of the Jewish ethos, among whom are Alix Kates Shulman, Jill Schary, Anne Roiphe, Judith Rossner, Ingrid Bengis, Nora Ephron, Vivian Gornick, Renata Adler, Carolyn Heilbrun, Gloria Steinem, and several more. Some are irrepressibly witty, others more serious, but in all of them there is an underlying irony which may flow from their sense of outsidedness, both as women and as Jews. More often than not, they have been uninvolved spectators— or, at best, participant observers—in a world where men have almost always assumed the principal roles, but perhaps that unwanted exclusion has given them that measure of detachment which is the *sine qua non* of genuine irony. As a friend of mine once remarked, "As soon as you machos give us a chance to be equally involved in all your affairs, we'll be just as big fools as you are. Meanwhile, we'll just go on watching you make asses of yourselves—and mostly envying your chance to do so."

But even when some of these women write about female protagonists (which most of them do) that aura of ironic detachment still persists, probably because their heroines are unavoidably confined within a masculine ambiance. For example, in *Memoirs of an Ex-Prom Queen*, Alix Kates Shulman's heroine retroactively realizes that the things that make a woman feel she has succeeded in a man's world are precisely the things that prevent her from doing so. Having been chosen queen of her high school prom ("the triumphs of the rest of my life were bound to seem anticlimactic"), Sasha Davis is envied by other girls and desired by all the males, but as she whirls around the dance floor with the star basketball player, her ecstasy is marred by the harsh intrusion of a male appraisal of her queenly status: "If you don't get in tonight, friend, you never will!" With this and numerous subsequent appraisals of feminine worth constantly influencing her own self-judgment, Sasha later doubts a college professor's praise of her term paper. Uncertain of her intellectual prowess but secure in her sexual power, she easily seduces him and symbolically says "with my body, I don't need a brain," thus rendering herself sexually exploitable and intellectually numb. She had long ago accepted the notion that female power is best expressed by giving oneself to a male lover. Thus, as an omnipotent prom queen, she had merely exercised *noblesse oblige* in letting the jock seduce her. The ultimate extension of such sexual submission can be seen in supposedly chic porno flicks in which female masochism is considered self-transcendence, and the women who can absorb the worst beating are presumed to be the most "sexually alive."

In Judith Rossner's *Looking for Mr. Goodbar* we see a woman whose emotions have been so deadened that she compulsively seeks violence as a kind of proof that she is still alive. Partially paralyzed by polio at the age of four and later immobilized for a year after spinal surgery for a condition her parents negligently ignored, Terry has suffered many additional traumas of a spiritual nature, but she has somehow learned to repress her mounting resentment. Then, after drifting into a series of bleak sure-to-fail contacts with various strangers, she becomes increasingly drawn to violent semicriminal types who would just as readily knife her as have sex with her. Intellectually contemptuous of less-educated lovers, she often goads them into a fury of sexual retaliation. Finally (indeed inevitably), she meets her nemesis, an unknown drifter she's picked up at a bar and taken home to her apartment. Suddenly, before he has been sexually satisfied, she orders him to leave, whereupon he beats her to death and has his orgasm inside her dying body.

Commenting on Rossner's protagonist, Ms. Hendin focuses on what seems to be an ever-recurring ambivalence in women who occasionally decide to be lions rather than lambs:

*Because she [Terry] is both self-punishing and destructive, she falls into an unselective aggressiveness that invites harsher retaliation. She guiltily seems to pursue a punishment that will keep her in her "place" and control her anger. What is being indicted is not aggressiveness, but the ambivalence and self-hatred that push the woman looking for a cure into the grave. . . . What all this suggests is that it is not enough for the lamb to behave like a lion; to be successful she has to be one.*

Unfortunately, Ms. Hendin's only example of a lamb becoming a lion is the fantasy transformation in Lois Gould's *A Sea-Change*, but she finally concludes that "We can become slaves of our dreams of power and permit our conflicted aggression to twist our lives."

## RAPE AND FANTASY

Molly Haskell in *Ms.* magazine comments:

*Brute force, as the first principle and last refuge of male supremacy, occupies a crucial place in our sexual consciousness. In a technological world where the exercise of physical strength is of a largely non-essential nature, the reassuring stereotypes of male physical superiority are more in demand than ever. The myth of the rapist-as-sexual-superman is one of these. It flourishes largely through a powerful unconscious resistance to the more accurate picture of the rapist as a sniveling, impotent, petty criminal.*

Rape and other forms of sexual violence have drawn increasing attention within the Women's Liberation Movement, but only a few of the most militant feminists have gone to the extremes of Susan Brownmiller's flat-out contention that all men are rapists—not only now but through all recorded history. With such a vast number of violators, there would have to be millions of women sexually attacked every day, when, in fact, according to a *Newsweek* report, less than 2 percent of the female population has been or ever will be raped in their lifetime—though that is 2 percent too much. In writing *Against Our Will: Men, Women and Rape*, Ms. Brownmiller may have intended to define rape in extremely broad terms, but in the final rendering her indictment is quite specific and unequivocally damning. There are no gray areas in her prose, no recognition of the ambivalent nature of most social intercourse. Using the other side of the Mailer-Miller coin, she seems determined to politicize sex into a male-female war of endless attrition.

Consequently, she is ready to cry "rape" in circumstances that might seem nothing more than a desired seduction to another woman. Take, for example, the widely divergent reactions of feminists to Lina Wertmuller's *Swept Away*. Some saw it as an offensive affirmation of the macho premise that "the rich bitch wanted to be forced into submission." Others (including Wertmuller herself) perceived the sexual episode as a poor man's victory over a spoiled-rich oppressor who had deliberately humiliated him, then subconsciously welcomed his retaliation. Still others, much less attuned to the politics of sex, were inclined to the simpler notion that when people are sexually drawn to each other at the right time and the right place, class distinctions are irrelevant—at least temporarily. There were other reactions, of course, running the gamut from praise to protest, all of which lead to the ancient premise—so aptly illustrated in *Rashamon*—that quite often people see the same things differently.

On the other hand, one cannot ignore the fact that real

rape is often glossed over and actually condoned in movies and in literature. One glaring example was Sam Peckinpah's *Straw Dogs*, in which a gang of hoodlums, feeling justifiably provoked by an openly sensual woman, began to rape her. She tries to fight them off for a while—then, true to the Hollywood credo that women crave brutal sex, the camera focuses on her hand relaxing its pressure against the rapist's shoulder, going limp for a moment, then passionately clutching his neck, suddenly converting unilateral violence into mutual lust. Quite obviously, says Peckinpah, she got not only what was coming to her *but what she wanted*.

In a subsequent panel discussion on rape, a male critic confidently asserted that this particular scene represented "a woman's fantasy," which prompted Molly Haskell to remind him that it was "a man's fantasy of a woman's fantasy." Ironically enough, it was a female psychoanalyst, Helen Deutsch, who provided the theoretical structure for much of the psychosocial mystique about female masochism and rape fantasy. An ardent disciple of Freud, who is constantly quoted in her two-volume *The Psychology of Women*, Deutsch solemnly insisted that the *desire* to be raped was the pivotal element of countless female daydreams, night dreams, adolescent and adult fantasies, wish fulfillments or fears—regardless of whether the women were normal and well-adjusted or borderline psychotics. Her analysis was based on the facile hypothesis that prehistoric woman was torn from her basic nature by the brute force of prehistoric man, thus forcing her to adapt to his sexual nature through chronic submission, so that rape fantasies were merely an echo of that ancient trauma. Consequently, as Haskell views it, "Instead of seeing in the peculiarities of women's fantasies a continued resistance to such a tyranny, Deutsch is determined to see women as actively embracing their sexual oppression." Haskell goes on to say that militants who insist that "real feminists" do not have rape fantasies are actually falling into a Deutschian trap of (1) identifying such fantasy as a neurosis to be combated, and (2) misinterpreting fantasy as something a woman wants to happen in real life. If this were so, one would have to assume that because men have castration anxieties, they want to be castrated—and that dreams of parents or children dying are symbolic wishes for their death—

whereas we fantasize such deaths or rape in order to prepare ourselves for the inevitable or the intolerable.

Considering how much women themselves disagree on whether they harbor a secret desire to be brutally violated, it is no small wonder that some men are willing to accept the most negative view. How, for example, should one react to the following passages from a short story by Jane Lazarre titled "A Subliminal Tale of Love and Sex," which appeared in *Ms.* magazine?

*For many years, I ignored the knowledge of what I loved in a man and instead, tirelessly obedient to social convention, I sought "The Punisher." And the more he rejected me during the hours of sunlight, the more likely I was, once it was dark and we began having sex, to come.*

· · ·

*She thought at times that she could easily sleep with other men, many of them, enjoying the special sexual style of a more punishing nature, and then return to him, fold into his gentleness, without the slightest feeling of disloyalty or breach of faith.*

· · ·

*The cruel lover would call and I, drawn to his touch and his body but unburdened by love, would go to him. Each time I performed, I was satisfied. And with that satisfaction, I was free, and dutifully went back to work.*

Whether certain women subconsciously desire brutality or whether they fantasize rape as a means of exorcising the very fear of it, the masochistic heroine is a constant figure in fiction written by women. Ultimately a male reader might begin to accept the Deutschian premise that subordination, submission and masochism are at the very core of the female psyche—and that it will require massive changes in our sociocultural norms to alter that negative condition. Among the most formidable obstacles are the tenets of various religions—Jewish, Catholic or Protestant in this country—and the following comment by the previously mentioned Marina Warner offers a hint of what Catholic women face in this regard:

*. . . [Long] after I had abandoned the Roman Catholic Church I still wanted to find out: What was this cult [of the Virgin Mary]? What was it I had worshipped? Particularly, I wanted to examine the paradox that a religion that accords the highest honor and love to a woman keeps women in a subordinate role,*

*that the countries where the Virgin is most powerful are also those where women have least mobility and influence in the public sphere, that in the celebration of the Ideal Woman, somehow humanity and women are both denigrated. . . . So on my way to Lourdes—aptly enough—I saw the Catholic cycle: Warnings against the perils of the flesh lead to obsession with it, which in turn increase desire. This, being sinful, inspires self-disgust, and leads therefore to a need for forgiveness, which only the sacraments of the church may grant. And the Virgin, who is holy because she overcame the flesh and yet gave birth, personifies that wheel on which Catholics are bound. . . . Thus men are emasculated by the importance they accord to women, and women lose access to existence outside the boundaries defined by the male.*

Although all women are bedeviled by male-dominated institutions, particularly Catholic and Orthodox Jewish women, the Women's Liberation Movement has effectively challenged some of the old rules and mandated bargains, and this ever-burgeoning revolution has been most notably evident in the realm of sex. The new feminist credo says "More and better orgasms for both sexes, more freedom to talk about sex in the most graphic terms, and anything goes between consenting adults of either gender." But men and women hear and read so much about multiple orgasms, clitoral stimulation, vaginal ache, premature ejaculation, swinging and sensate focus that they feel an enormous pressure to perform "better" and to enjoy sex as the books insist they should. Sometimes the pressure is open and direct; more often it is subtle and subliminal. In either case, the pressure too frequently becomes unbearable and debilitating, with impotence and orgasmic failure the inevitable result.

## THE NEW SEX ETHOS

Consequently, since the penis is more visible than the clitoris and since it is impossible to fake an erection, male anxiety has been one of the most prevalent aspects of our new sex ethos. Here, for example, is a fairly accurate description of this syndrome by Leonore Tiefer:

*Today many women are saying that it's not enough for a women to give; she also deserves to get. She can be an active and satisfied sex partner, not a passive flounder. This change impinges on the male, of course, for now it is not enough to be masculine by producing an erection; erections are necessary, but not sufficient. "How can I keep thrusting long enough for her to come?" men ask. "How long, for heaven's sake, is long enough?" "What am I supposed to do about the clitoris?" "If women can have more than one orgasm, how can I ever tell if she's had enough?" "How can I keep my erection going long enough for her to get aroused fully?" In the extreme case, the new demands may detract from a man's sense of masculinity and make him so uncertain that his fear conquers his desire.*

Although the balance of power within the bedroom has been radically changed for thousands of couples, with women ever more frequently assuming the dominant role, the balance of power in nonsexual activities has changed very little. In certain areas a token number of women have achieved at least a semblance of equality—in publishing and the broadcast media, for example—but their status in most occupations is still gallingly inequitable, giving rise to the kind of anger and frustration one sees in magazine articles such as "Phallic Imperialism: Why Economic Recovery Will Not Work For Us" by Andrea Dworkin:

*Fucking is the means by which the male colonializes the female, whether or not the intended goal is impregnation (reproduction). Fucking authenticates marriage and, in or out of marriage, it is regarded as an act of possession. The possessor is the one with a phallus; the possessed is the one without a phallus. Society in both capitalist and socialist countries (including China) is organized so as to guarantee the imperial right of each man to fuck at least one woman.*

*. . .*

*In male supremacist cultures, women are believed to embody carnality; women are sex. A man wants what a woman has—sex. He can steal it (rape), persuade her to give it away (seduction), rent it (prostitution), lease it over the long term (marriage in the United States), or own it outright (marriage in most societies). A man can do some or all of the above, over and over again.*

The trend toward such stridency and linguistic excess continues unabated, particularly in matters related to sex, with some writers indulging in categorical condemnations that reflect more anger than sense ("all men are . . . all females demand. . . "). For example, the *Village Voice* published an article in November 1976, titled "Sissyhood Is Powerful," in which Frank Rose flatly stated that "Jews are seen as pussy-whipped from birth, and anxious besides." To which one reader, D.H. Blum, immediately responded in a short letter-to-editor which was partly tongue in cheek: " . . . I am very anxious to know exactly who is doing the seeing and where are they standing. Pussy-whipped from birth? For the record, I was *not* pussy-whipped from birth. It didn't begin until about the first grade."

As one might expect, such male-female conflicts are sometimes exacerbated by hints of racial resentment. In a review of a novel by Gayl Jones for *Esquire* magazine (December 1976 issue), D. Keith Mano compared two of her books and found them repetitious and banal, and was not too impressed either by one of the heroines' unique revenge on a lover, whose penis she bit off with a sudden chomp of her strong white teeth. Perhaps identifying with the castrated ex-lover, Mano proceeded to lambast the black author's second novel in no uncertain terms:

*The practical truth is, if* Corregidora *had been written, say, by some white first novelist, it would still be in manuscript. Moreover, Jones' thudding, remorseless sensuality would have seemed a libel against all blacks. But when blacks write about blacks we accept their information, rather as we accept anthropological studies of Africa: they are a different race; they have their quaint customs; this isn't vulgar or repetitive, it's ethnic. . . . We tend to think that [black] women writing about sex have a new, ethnic point of view: real, authoritative; heck, even* sociological. *So men write reviews for* Corregidora *that say '[her] insights into the woman's psyche [are] rare in American fiction' . . . But if a white man's* Corregidora *had been published, well, write the reviews yourself. 'Mr. X is a sick racist who imagines that black people are obsessed with sex. . . .'*

Whatever the merits of this particular case, one can easily foresee that certain men and women are determined to fight the male-female war to the bitter end, and neither will hesitate to use any weapons available, from scorn to insult to whimsy. One can only hope that humor will be the saving grace.

# 11
# Conclusion

No aspect of our lives is more confusing, more troubling or more controversial than sex. And anyone who seeks to theorize about any facet of sexual behavior must surely expect a virtual cross fire of mild to hostile criticism, particularly if he or she ventures to view sex through a prism of culture and religion. But prompted by a long-held conviction that culture and religion are among the most powerful influences in shaping our erotic habits and attitudes, I have accepted the risks of presenting the results of a prolonged inquiry that has fascinated, confused and amused me for several years.

As my interviews have repeatedly revealed, it is often difficult to pinpoint the exact influence of such phenomena as an Irish Catholic's sense of sin or the dimensions of a Jewish bachelor's ironic machismo—but such factors most assuredly impinge upon their conduct in bed. Whether direct or indirect, conscious or subconscious, our religious upbringing and ethnic backgrounds play vital roles in our approach to (or retreat from) sex, even for those of us who have abandoned our childhood religion or who have moved away from our original ethnic enclaves.

As for those critics who may question the data herein or the manner by which it was obtained, I would simply observe that is has always been difficult (perhaps impossible) to get a truly accurate assessment of sexual behavior, because such information is necessarily subjective. Since direct observation is seldom possible, one must rely on what people say about their personal sex lives—and there is a wide variance in the degree of candor one can expect in any kind of interview. Some people tell outright lies, others exaggerate or minimize and some are probably unable to report accurately because they may not know how they feel about sex or, because of some psychic block, are unaware of this or that aberration in their erotic behavior. Certain people, of course, simply refuse to discuss personal matters with anyone—nothing being more personal than sex—while others will freely discuss anything about themselves or anyone close to them.

Consequently, no matter how well structured a survey may be, I think that it is quixotic to expect accurate, unchallengeable statistical data about any aspect of sex. More than thirty years ago, when Alfred Kinsey and his associates produced their monumental studies on male and female sexual behavior, scores of social scientists poked holes in almost all the statistics cited therein. As one Harvard scholar pointed out, "The most generous comment one can make about these books is that the statistics reflect the sexual conduct and feelings of those few Americans who were willing to talk. As for the vast majority of the population, Kinsey's numerical data is probably meaningless."

Yet Kinsey and his colleagues did perform certain valuable functions, one of which was to validate the open inquiry into the hidden side of the American psyche. And though countless other surveys, such as the Hite Report, have suffered from a similar statistical unreliability, they too have added valuable insights into the *eros* and *ethos* of our society. I trust that my efforts may be viewed in that light.